O9-ABH-737

WITHDRAWAL

Career Launcher

Hospitality

Career Launcher series

Career Launcher

Hospitality

Kirsten Hall and Christian Schulz

Ferguson Publishing
An imprint of Infobase Publishing

Career Launcher: **Hospitality**

Copyright © 2011 by Infobase Publishing, Inc.

Ferguson
An imprint of Infobase Publishing
132 West 31st Street
New York NY 10001

Library of Congress Cataloging-in-Publication Data

Hall, Kirsten and Schulz, Christian.
    Hospitality / Kirsten Hall and Christian Schulz.
        p. cm. — (Career launcher)
    Includes bibliographical references and index.
    ISBN-13: 978-0-8160-7971-1 (hardcover : alk. paper)
    ISBN-10: 0-8160-7971-4 (hardcover : alk. paper)
1. Hospitality industry—Vocational guidance. I.
Schulz, Christian (Christian Dahl) II. Title.
    TX911.3.V62H35 2010
    647.94'023—dc22

                                                                2010012106

Produced by Print Matters, Inc.
Text design by A Good Thing, Inc.
Cover design by Takeshi Takahashi
Cover printed by Art Print Company, Taylor, PA
Book printed and bound by Maple Press, York, PA
Date printed: November 2010

Printed in the United States of America

10 9 8 7 6 5 4 3 2 1

This book is printed on acid-free paper.

Contents

Foreword

Hospitality is defined as "the friendly reception and treatment of guests or strangers." In ancient Greece, people working in hospitality were expected to take in strangers, wash their feet, and treat them as members of their own families by providing food, lodging, transportation, safety, and whatever else they might require. This sounds like a full-time job to me, and in contemporary times, that is exactly what it has become.

While it is still common in some cultures to graciously invite strangers into homes and care for them accordingly, in these times it would be foolhardy to travel to a new city with the false hope that all of your needs would be attended to by generous citizens ready to welcome you into their homes for as long as you would like to stay. It is not that such an environment is unavailable to travelers—but it must be arranged, paid for, and left in the hands of the qualified and willing people who have made hospitality their livelihood.

The hospitality industry is immense and worldwide. Hospitality companies include hotels, resorts, casinos, restaurants—and all of the services that these companies provide. Jobs in the hospitality industry that might first come to mind include hotel front desk manager, concierge, bellman, restaurant server, pool or beach attendant, and any other person with whom you might come into direct contact during a hotel stay.

But hospitality jobs also include those positions that are less visible to the guest, yet who work just as hard to positively impact a guest's stay. A hotel's general manager, food and beverage director, landscaper, prep kitchen line cook, laundry attendant, or engineer might not be someone with whom you will necessarily come face to face during your stay, but their work and actions are sure to affect your experience.

Because there are so many different types of service a guest might potentially need, the opportunities for a career in hospitality are limitless. There are not many careers that you cannot apply to hospitality. Aside from the obvious hotel careers, any restaurant, spa, accounting, and IT vocation is also utilized in the hospitality industry. Studying to be a marine biologist or chemist? I bet there are plenty of resorts in the Bahamas, Las Vegas, and Dubai in need of a person just like yourself who can maintain the pH levels in their sting ray tanks.

And so the opportunities are there—and the benefits are rewarding. Most resorts and hotels are part of national or international corporations. If you are hired into a large corporation and prove yourself to be a valuable employee, the sky is the limit in terms of opportunity. You have the prospect of transferring jobs within that same hotel, or even to another hotel held by the same company. Ever wanted to know what it is like to live in Chicago? How about Berlin? Or perhaps Bali? Even if you are not interested in making such a big change, most large corporations offer minimum employee rates for stays at their other properties. This would give you the opportunity to take affordable vacations during which you could experience the same level of hospitality that you have been accustomed to providing.

I run a restaurant in a hotel. The restaurant is a joint venture between the international hotel group and an international restaurant management company. If I suddenly felt like exploring other employment possibilities, the first places I would look would be within both companies. I would have many options, since I would likely be one of the first candidates considered for opening positions (as I am already employed by the companies).

Fortunately for you, the hospitality field is relatively easy to get into. I work with people who trained in school before entering the industry as well as others who schooled themselves through experience. Those who graduate from prestigious programs are impressive candidates because they are knowledgeable of all of the latest trends and programs in the industry. They are generally younger and attain upper management positions in less time than those simply working their way up.

It is a pleasure to work with these trained professionals because they have been taught the most recent technological tools and are able to complete tasks quickly and easily. And they can assist the rest of the team by sharing their expertise. I always enjoy working with people with hospitality educations because I learn from them on a daily basis. I, on the other hand, took the other route to management. I majored in English in college. While my choice of majors may not have prepared me for a specific career, the skill of writing well is universally helpful in any occupation.

While in college, I held my first restaurant job as a hostess. After graduation I fell back on the ease and monetary reward of waitressing. I had a no-stress job that paid well. Then I bartended for a while, after which I concluded that waiting tables was more for me. My employers always asked me to consider a management position, but I knew that promotion to management would result in earning less money, so I always declined. While some hospitality positions are attractive because of the ease with which tips are earned, you should always keep in mind that this is the first industry to be affected in an economic downturn. I realized the importance of a guaranteed income in the form of a salary when the tourists stopped coming to New York City after the events of September 11. Luckily, my employer had remained interested in offering me a management position—and here I am, eight years later, very happy to be on salary. (If you work for a luxury hotel, fewer of your guests will be affected by economic recessions, but even the best in the industry will feel the effects.)

Whether you choose to pursue your hospitality career via academia or experience, it is wise to continue learning every day. Observe your coworkers and superiors. Emulate their strengths and be sure to avoid adopting their weaknesses. Try to learn anything anyone has to teach. This, more than anything else, has been my key to success.

Of course, it is important to learn the tools of the trade and to figure out your career objectives—but first and foremost in this industry is the guest. Without guests, we would not be in business. In any hotel, you will learn to engage your guests. Some hotels will provide you with scripts to use while others will simply want you to be yourself. However you may approach hospitality, it comes down to making the guest feel at home and eager to return.

You must learn how, if you do not already know, to read people. A single traveler, staying for a business obligation might have entirely different expectations of hotel staff than a group of girls in town for a bachelorette weekend. It will be your job to decipher (if not intuit) the needs of your guests, to adapt to their expectations, and to ensure that each and every guest has the best stay possible.

And now I wish you the best *read* possible. Best of luck to you—and welcome to the industry!

—Julia Hanan
Manager, The Blue Door Restaurant at the Delano Hotel,
Miami, Florida

Acknowledgments

The authors would like to thank Sharmilla Araya for her thorough research and insight, without which this writing would not have been possible. We further acknowledge the invaluable contributions of Thomas Sullivan, Julia Hanan, Kate DeCosta, Cara Lane, and Patrick Byrne.

Introduction

A career in the hospitality industry can be both challenging and rewarding. It can try your patience, fray your nerves, and test your spirit. But it will also afford you the opportunity to work with creative and interesting people in an environment that is fast-paced and almost never boring. Now that you have chosen to pursue a career in this field, it is in your best interest to gain the greatest possible understanding of the industry as a whole, its different sectors, and the specific positions within each sector. Anyone truly interested in moving up the ranks should become familiar with the history, trends, and vocabulary that are unique to the world of hospitality. *Career Launcher: Hospitality* will provide you with everything you need to know to think, talk, and act like a pro from your first day on the job.

The hospitality industry comprises a broad spectrum of diverse businesses that offer myriad opportunities for advancement and lateral movement. Included within the hospitality industry are specialized facilities, such as theme parks and museums. Yet the vast majority of employees in this field work in either accommodations or food and beverage service. To address the ins-and-outs of every hospitality job would result in a tome rivaling the phone book in thickness. This book will train its focus primarily on the industry's two major sectors.

The primary responsibilities for those who work in the hotel and lodging sector include making sure that guests' needs are attended to, their accommodations are comfortable, and that general hotel operations are running smoothly. The United States is home to more than 60,000 lodging establishments, ranging from small boutique hotels to internationally renowned resorts. With so many types of establishments to choose from, careful consideration must be paid to finding the type of establishment that best suits your personality and interests.

The restaurant and food service sector offers unrivaled potential for promotion. With hard work and determination, it is not unheard of for a worker starting out as a prep cook to eventually rise to the position of executive chef. This sector is one of the nation's largest employers. Many young adults start their professional lives here and discover that, with effort, focus, and additional education, a rewarding career path is available to those with a strong work ethic.

How to Use This Book

The purpose of this book is to help you make the most of your career in the hospitality industry. In the following six chapters, you will find a comprehensive overview of the industry as well as advice on working your way up the ladder of success. Read all six chapters for a complete industry education or simply refer to individual chapters for discussions of particular topics.

Chapter 1 traces the origins of hospitality as well as its evolution over time. Inns and eateries have been around almost as long as human civilization itself, taking various forms based on differences in ethnicity, politics, and geography. To understand an industry that has been so long subjected to the vagaries of cultural influence, it is important to note which developments have been retained over time, and which have been discarded. Chapter 1 highlights the industry's major advances as well as the external influences that contributed to them.

Chapter 2 provides a numbers-driven overview of the hospitality industry's current state of affairs. This section offers statistics on employment, wages, profits, current and possible future trends, technology, key conferences and industry events, major players and industry forces, and issues of law and government regulation. Not surprisingly, hotels and restaurants are subject to close governmental scrutiny, so scrupulous knowledge of the relevant statutes and codes is necessary to avoid potential pitfalls.

Chapter 3 describes in detail the various jobs within the hospitality industry. There is a great variety of professions in this field, and the performance of each must mesh perfectly with the others in order to keep the larger operation running smoothly. The complexity of a restaurant or hotel's system is largely unknown to the general public. For example, a novice might believe "chef" to be a single position. Rather, within the category of "chef" there are over a dozen separate occupations including executive chef, sous chef, chef de partie, line cook, and prep cook. This professional hierarchy, with its coordinated individual roles, has evolved through trial and error into one system that is employed almost universally. Only thorough familiarity with everyone's roles can a team function as a cohesive unit. This section also details potential routes for advancement by detailing the chain of command which exists between the various positions.

In Chapter 4, you will find a roadmap for success within the industry's individual professions as well as more general advice that can be applied to practically any professional endeavor. This includes sections on job training and continuing education, job searching, interview techniques, dealing with bosses and co-workers, and even a brief discussion of entrepreneurism for those considering opening their own establishments.

Chapter 5 provides a glossary of terms that will help you to successfully communicate with your coworkers. As with many industries, hospitality has evolved a unique vocabulary to describe the people, places, and things specific to it. From the finest five-star restaurant to your local neighborhood greasy spoon, there are many words and phrases in common use that are completely foreign to those outside the know.

Chapter 6 contains an extensive collection of Web sites, books, and films that provide useful information about the industry and offer a glimpse behind the curtain at the reality of working at a modern-day hotel or restaurant.

Within each chapter, you will notice the following boxed features, which will augment your understanding of a particular topic:

→ **Best Practices:** These will tell you how to improve your efficiency and performance in the workplace. Though most are aimed at the hospitality world specifically, others are general hints for professional success regardless of industry.

→ **Everyone Knows:** These highlight invaluable information that everyone in the hospitality industry must have at his or her fingertips.

→ **Fast Facts:** These are interesting and handy tidbits that will enhance your understanding of the field as a whole. They will also provide an opportunity to impress colleagues and superiors with your breadth of knowledge.

→ **Keeping In Touch:** These items offer strategies for effective business communication—whether via e-mail, over the phone, or in person.

→ **On the Cutting Edge:** These sidebars examine emerging industry trends. With their focus on the latest tendencies and innovations, these will prove especially useful to those considering moving to new positions within the field.

→ **Problem Solving:** These features present hypothetical circumstances that may present themselves to someone working in this unpredictable business as well as tips for navigating these scenarios.

➡ **Professional Ethics:** Irrespective of industry, a strong ethical base is fundamental for successful career growth. These items create hypothetical dilemmas and suggest paths to their successful resolution.

No matter what your educational background or previous professional experience, the possibilities for employment and growth within the service industry are almost boundless. This book will serve as your secret weapon, guiding you along your career path and providing the information you will need to maximize your opportunities for success.

Chapter 1

Industry History

For thousands of years, humans have worked together on activities intrinsic to their survival: the gathering and planting of food, the building of shelters, the protection of their young, and migration from one place to another. The act of travel is as ancient as humanity itself—and so is the need for hospitable places for those seeking food and shelter.

Early trade routes sustained the Greek, Chinese, and Roman economies. In the 1400s, the silk and spice trades help foster tremendous growth of European and Eastern markets, creating demand for places to rest during periods of travel. The modern-day businessman, who often travels and stays at hotels, and who frequents bars and restaurants in foreign lands, is more similar to Marco Polo than he may realize.

Business remains the same today—it is still conducted in lounges, barrooms, and restaurants all over the world.

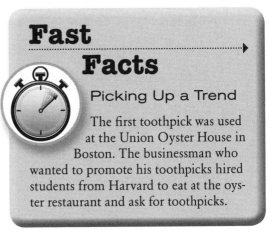

Fast Facts

Picking Up a Trend

The first toothpick was used at the Union Oyster House in Boston. The businessman who wanted to promote his toothpicks hired students from Harvard to eat at the oyster restaurant and ask for toothpicks.

And just as successful as the marriage of business and pleasure is the joining of food and drink establishments—it is hard to imagine they were once separate. However, early taverns served only food, early restaurants served strong drink, and "coffeehouses" served neither. As you read more about the history of taverns, restaurants, and public houses, you will see the emergence of an industry willing to change in whichever ways necessary to make a profit and satisfy the palate of the customer.

Hospitality in the Ancient World

The simplest inns emerged in the first century A.D. These inns consisted of walled-in areas constructed around wells. Larger inns had separate rooms surrounding central courtyards. At simpler inns, animal owners stayed with their livestock. Inns were a common site in the regions eventually conquered by the Greeks and Romans.

In Hebrew, the word *mawlone* referred to an inn, or lodging. *Mawlone* could also mean places where large military forces, or groups of people traveling together, stayed at night. Ancient inns were typically found near sources of ground water and often relied on wells dug in nearby areas. Lodging and care of animals was free.

In the Middle East, inns were called *manzil* or, as the Persians referred to them, *khans* (caravans). Travelers stayed at no cost (in terms of currency). However, food and water required payment. In Asia Minor, around the same time, travelers would stay along the trade routes in places called *locandos*. These roughly constructed buildings dotted the landscape throughout the Middle East. They were made up of rooms that were much like compartments that circled courtyards. In Egypt, owners of these establishments were the first to brew beer. Women often took care of these inns, which were considered houses of "ill-repute."

By 500 B.C., inns were commonplace in Greece. National festivals and games drew large throngs of people to particular areas, where inns with comfortable quarters awaited guests of both foreign and native descent. A *proxinoi* was a Greek whose job it was to help citizens with directions, tickets, or with finding a place to stay. He also helped visitors with any legal problems experienced during their stay.

In ancient Greece, citizens often met for wine and conversation during events called symposia. While drinking strong wine out of bowls, they engaged in discourse about art, politics, and philosophy. Much later, Romans who were considered learned men held forums called *convivia*. Convivium hosts sent invitations to small groups of important citizens and served them wine during an evening of provocative conversation. The Romans were somewhat more progressive than the Greeks, allowing women the opportunity to occasionally attend.

The Romans improved upon the idea of the inn, ultimately dividing it according to its purposes: drinking places and resting places. The drinking establishments were called *taberna diversoria*. Entertainment became a mainstay at many of the *taberna*. Guests were entertained with live acts performed by musicians quietly strumming on the lyre, jugglers, acrobats, clowns (who also told raunchy stories), and philosophers who posed tricky, logical, or epistemological questions. Strippers and prostitutes were available for hire. Flute girls and dancing girls were considered the most popular of all live acts and were prized by the taverns.

Lore about ancient Rome holds that the *vomitorium* was a room where guests would retreat in order to induce vomiting before continuing to eat and drink. However, the existence of such places has been doubted by some scholars. Instead it seems that, while there may indeed have been a place called a *vomitorium*, it was not a place where people went to vomit. Rather, the *vomitorium* was a large passageway within the Coliseum in Rome—an amphitheater that held up to 50,000 people—designed to move masses of people between tiers and seats. The rapid movement of so many people at once likely gave birth to its name. Still, it is undisputable that the Romans did indeed have the habit of inducing vomit, as servants often stood ready to collect the waste of the guests.

In 2004, German scientists unearthed a 2,000-year-old roadside inn in Nuess, Germany. The property consisted of a hotel, a restaurant, and a chariot service. The theory is that this roadside eatery was probably one of many along the Roman Long Road—a well-known trade route that linked the North Sea coast to southern Italy—on which scholars think these types of resting places could be found roughly 20 miles apart (horses needed rest, food, and water every 20 miles). Chariot riders relied on carriage maintenance service available along the way. Travelers would be offered meals consisting of rice, lentils, chicken, and pork and served with wine. Sweet cakes made with almonds and sesame seeds were dessert. The hotel/restaurant/chariot shop was very large, probably in an effort to attract travelers. Much like today's large billboard ads on highways, the goal was likely to entice visitors to stay and refuel. Remains of these roads can still be seen today, and some modern European motorways still follow the original road designed by Roman engineers over 1,500 years ago.

Roman garrisons were posted along the routes to ensure safe passage of travelers. These inns were actually paid for out of public funds and were constructed by the Roman government, subject to regulation by the same. Some of these inns became famously known as destination vacation spots and were considered some of the best watering holes in the region.

Roman law required an innkeeper, his servants, and his family to be held responsible for the property of the guests while they stayed at the hotel—unless the damage caused was due to an act of God (*damnum fatale*) or the King's enemies (*vis major*).

Hospitality: the Middle Ages to the Nineteenth Century

The concept of people eating outside of their homes occurred in the East much earlier than in the West. Eating establishments have been in operation in China since the seventh century. These early restaurants catered to the local palette as well as travelers who passed through the region. Teahouses and taverns were popular with a growing middle class, and food orders were customized according to the desires of customers. Historians agree that the growth of restaurants, theaters, gambling dens, and prostitution rings combined with one million Chinese people, their culture of hospitality, and a viable paper currency led to a time of great prosperity in China. Ma Yu Chicken Bucket house is a restaurant that opened in 1153 A.D. in Kaifeng, China, and that has miraculously survived wars, invasions, and dynasty changes throughout the centuries—still serving bucket chicken today!

Chinese eateries arrived in the West and sprang up all over California when Chinese immigrants first arrived in the mid-nineteenth century. Chinese workers came to work on the American railroads and to pan for gold in the California goldmines. "Chow-chows" were Chinese restaurants that could be found in Chinatowns all over California. Marked with triangular yellow cloths at their entrances, chow-chows quickly gained in popularity with other immigrant populations arriving in the West. They are now considered a staple in American culture with local Chinese restaurants in every part of the United States.

Restaurants as a place where customers could enjoy prepared dishes appeared throughout the medieval Islamic world even before the Far East. The notion of a three-course meal was developed in

Islamic Spain in the ninth century. A brilliant and successful businessman named Ziryab conceived "courses" in which diners could experience different dishes (such as soup, a main, or dessert) one at a time. Obviously, this idea still influences the modern food service industry today.

During the Middle Ages in Europe, monks were responsible for the care of weary travelers in their monasteries. People from nobility or who held rank were offered respite in the house itself, while those of lesser means settled for the chambers. These chambers (which consisted of a hall and sleeping rooms) were used as "great halls" before guests went to sleep. An officer of importance, such as a knight, would eat at the upper end of the great hall (also known as the dais) and also had his own sleeping quarters. His servants sat at the lower end of the hall for their meals and slept on the floor after the meal was over and the tables had been pushed aside. Hospices were built to host pilgrims and could be found in the Swiss Alps and on roads leading to the Holy Land and other famous religious shrines. Monks were famous for making excellent beer, which they served to travelers (but also consumed themselves).

A growing middle class in Europe no longer wanted to stay in abbeys and monasteries, instead preferring more luxurious accommodations. In the fourteenth century, this led to the development of inns, taverns, and alehouses in England and Scotland, which advertised their businesses by suspending long poles above their doors and wrapping vines around them with accompanying signs. Signs with illustrations served as advertising for those who could not read.

In France in 1765 a shrewd businessman named Boulanger hung a sign outside his tavern advertising a dish made of sheep's fat in white sauce. He called it a *restaurant*, which is derived from the French word meaning "to restore." At the time, almost all food dishes were prepared off the premises and delivered to the tavern. Guilds controlled the monopoly of certain food items: *tamisiers* made bread; *patissiers* prepared poultry, pies, and tarts; and *vinaigriers* made sauces. These food items were sent to the taverns without any input from owners as to what they might want to serve their customers. A tavern's business, it was assumed, was to provide drink and lodging—and the business of food was up to the guilds that controlled the preparation and delivery of it. Because Boulanger disputed the status quo and prepared food at his own tavern, legal action was taken against him. He was sued by the guilds, which claimed he was infringing upon their right to sell prepared food. Boulanger argued that his patrons were not only travelers looking for rest and drink but also local citizens who wanted meals according to their wishes. He won the suit and this triumph marked the beginning of a new industry—the restaurant. Subsequently, this new type of inn/tavern/restaurant began to spring up all over Europe.

"Coffeehouses" also became popular meeting places for businesspeople in London. In the 1700s, Lloyd's coffeehouse was considered the place to do business among merchant marine men and maritime insurance agents. In 1771, this "coffeehouse" came under the ownership of insurance underwriters, and became Lloyd's of London's—the oldest and most prestigious insurance underwriting firm in the Western world. More evidence that business and pleasure do indeed mix.

Another well-known and long-standing type of tavern is the Irish pub, which was once the cultural center of Irish life. Irish pubs were constructed from stone and often featured roughly-built, wooden furniture. Large fireplaces added warmth and comfort. They served ale and traditional Irish fare, including Cornish pastry (meat baked into a dough), shepherd's pie (meat with twice cooked mashed potatoes), steak and kidney pie, bangers and mash (pan-fried sausage with mashed potatoes and gravy), and Yorkshire pudding (also known as "toad in the hole"). The Irish also made their pubs places for songs, stories, gossip, and rumors. In the nineteenth century, the Irish pub was outlawed under the oppressive British rule—seen as meeting grounds for those who opposed the British. Still, Irish pubs continued to flourish and served as a haven where frustrations could be vented and rebellions planned.

A Brief History of American Inns and Taverns

The inn and tavern have each served a special role in American history, from the time of the revolution to the present day.

Early American Taverns

Just as in seventeenth-century Europe, colonial America had many of its own public houses, or taverns, where men gathered for beer and conversation. Meals were available at these taverns—but the customer had little input into what he was eating or how it was prepared. Taverns in colonial America, like churches and other public spaces, held cultural and political significance for the citizenry at the time. It has often been said that the headquarters of the American Revolution were the many taverns that flourished in the thirteen colonies.

America's inns and taverns served as places to obtain both meals and drinks, and they sometimes offered crude lodgings. In fact, early American taverns and inns were the only means to public food, drink, and lodging. It was not until 1827 that the first fine dining establishment opened in New York City and the concept of food as the "focus of the event" was born. Inns and taverns had more historical relevance for America than restaurants and hotels, which are more modern inventions.

Early Dutch settlers established taverns in Manhattan in the 1600s. The Staadt Herberg (or, as translated from Dutch, "City Tavern"), was one of the first taverns built in 1642, on Pearl Street. It was constructed of solid stone and stood three stories tall. Governor William Kieft, who needed a place for visitors to stay when they called upon him from abroad, constructed it. It later became the City Hall. The travelers of the Dutch West India Company were its primary guests, and it was said to have only served liquors and beers from the West India Company.

When the British took over in Manhattan, they established two new taverns: The King's Arms and The Province Arms. The King's Arms changed names on several occasions, becoming first the City Arms, then Burn's Coffee House, and thirdly Cape's Tavern. Local British government officials saw the need to regulate the sale of liquors and spirits as well as to provide food and lodging for traveling folk. Laws were put on the books that determined the opening of some kind of public house in each early colonial town or village. Regulation of alcohol soon followed. The habit of "bar hopping" may have originated with a law that stated that anyone found sitting idle and drunk in a tavern for more than half an hour would lead to a landlord fine.

Fraunces' Tavern at 54 Pearl Street in New York City was known as a common meeting place while City Hall was under construction. Congress met there often and it is known as the site where George Washington gave his famous farewell speech to the Continental Army. Fraunces' Tavern remained in business until the early 1900s. The Sons of the Revolution purchased the tavern in 1904 and had an architect restore the building. It remains as a museum today and still houses the old tavern.

Another tavern that has earned a special place in American history is Montaigne's Tavern in New York City. It was the headquarters for the Sons of Liberty, an organization of working class men who rebelled against British rule. A special dinner was held at Montaigne's to celebrate the repeal of the Stamp Act in 1766.

Samuel Adams plotted the Boston Tea Party at the Green Dragon Tavern in Boston's North End. Patrick Henry, who gave the famous "Give me liberty or give me death" speech, organized the Virginia legislature with his colleagues at the Raleigh Tavern in Williamsburg.

Taverns continued to have historical significance throughout New England. Buckman Tavern in Lexington, Massachusetts, was built in 1710 and was a popular gathering place for the colonial minutemen. On April 19, 1775, minutemen waited at the tavern for the arrival of the British as announced by Paul Revere. A single shot fired on the Common signaled the beginning of the American Revolution. The tavern was later restored by the Lexington Historical Society and is a museum today.

The Declaration of Independence and the Constitution were conceived in the pubs and taverns of Philadelphia. The City Tavern in Philadelphia was a popular watering hole for the delegates of the constitutional convention. The First and Second Continental Congresses met on Saturdays to have dinner at the tavern. George Washington, Thomas Jefferson, Benjamin Franklin, and John Adams all frequented the tavern during the time that the Constitution was being written. The City Tavern continues to be in existence and still has a menu today that features a cuisine inspired by dishes from the eighteenth century.

As with all early American business conducted at taverns, the slave trade was no different. In Boston, a tavern known as Bunch-Of-Grapes sold beer, tickets to performances, and slaves. As slave-buyers did business along the busy King Street, they often ended up meeting business associates at the Bunch-Of-Grapes for food, drink, and slave sales. It was known as a Whig tavern, and one of the first Masonic lodges. In 1793 it was demolished.

Aside from the political significance of taverns in early American history, taverns were an important part of rural American culture. Men's per capita consumption of alcohol was high all over the new country. The estimated alcohol consumption of each male adult was about six gallons of pure alcohol per year—double the consumption of alcohol of the American adult in 1985. Judges, lawyers, doctors, blacksmiths, farmers, and laborers met regularly to drink a dram at a tavern. On Sundays, the taverns were open at noon and there were paths that led from the churches or Sunday meetinghouses straight to the taverns. There they would remain until it was time for the afternoon services, when they would make their way back to church.

The Temperance Movement

Many churches began to oppose the use of alcohol, and the habit of drinking at taverns before Sunday afternoon meetings soon waned. Many tavern-keepers began to serve lemonade and coffee instead of liquor. Smoking declined and arguments once fueled by alcohol use declined. The New England drinking culture was beginning to change. Many towns witnessed the erection of temperance hotels across from traditional taverns. These hotels served coffee. Temperance workers wanted to control the sale and use of alcohol, even though they believed drunkenness could not be cured. Bosses could no longer give their workers alcohol on the job. (This practice was abolished in 1870.) Still, however, drinking continued on the job— and drunkenness continued to be a problem, even among the community leaders.

When the medical profession joined the temperance movement, drunkenness was accepted as a disease. Samuel Woodward, a physician at the time, described alcoholism as a psychological dependence with a physical symptoms of withdrawal. Temperance workers argued that the legal system encouraged and supported the sale and use of alcohol to a level that was detrimental to the morals of the communities. Armed with religious fervor and support, the early temperance movement found a foothold in American culture.

Taverns after the Civil War

During the Civil War the temperance movement waned as the proponents of temperance turned their focus to abolishing slavery. Initially, rations of beer were given to troops but this practice was stopped mid-way through the war as war revenue became scarce. Recognizing an emerging market, local beer salesmen followed the troops throughout the country. The American government recognized an opportunity to make money that could be used to pay off a growing war debt. The Internal Revenue Service was authorized to tax the salesmen at a dollar a barrel.

What Americans drank changed with mass immigration from Germany and other European countries. Between 1850 and 1970, beer consumption increased from 1.6 gallons to 3.8 gallons per person, per year. Even though consumption rose, lower-alcohol-content beers were being brewed. German beer taverns flourished in German-American communities and served as social centers for the entire family: men, women, and children. Sundays at German taverns found German immigrants dancing to lively music and enjoying other popular entertainment. Moderate use of alcohol was strongly encouraged.

When America moved west, the saloon became the social center of the drinking culture. Brown's Saloon near the Wyoming/Utah/Colorado border was established in 1882. Large mining towns such as Dodge City, Kansas, and Livingston, Montana, watched as their saloons flourished due to frequent patronage from cowboys and miners.

Everyone Knows

The Importance of Signs

Hospitality signing is often intrinsic to success. For no business is this more important than the motel. A sign conveys the special ambience offered by a particular facility, which is why the most effective signs are custom designed and crafted to complement a building's architecture, offering a statement of quality and professionalism to patrons and passers-by. Motel signs, in all of their beauty and variation, have assumed a permanent place in Americana.

Saloons remained popular throughout the 1800s and early 1900s. All kinds of saloons came into existence: restaurant saloons, dance hall saloons (featuring saloon girls and prostitutes), card game saloons, billiards saloons. Yet the drinking saloon was always the favorite. Many of the concoctions served at saloons were made by mixing whiskey with whatever was available: gunpowder, tobacco, burnt sugar, ammonia, or anything else on hand. For those with weaker hearts and stomachs, beer was an option.

The temperance moved west as women moved out to the new, harsh country and were often left to fend for themselves after their husbands died from alcoholism. One such unfortunate widow was Carrie Amelia Nation, who lost her first husband to alcoholism. She was known to smash saloons and liquor stores with rocks and hatchets as she declared, "Men, I have come to save you from a drunkard's fate." As crime escalated, alcohol became the chief culprit to be blamed. The movement took its mission seriously as it sought to protect the women and children who they saw as the victims of hapless husbands who drank themselves to death. Temperance workers also sought to ban alcohol in the workplace and eliminate drinking during lunch periods.

Prohibition

In the beginning of the twentieth century, temperance organizations were vibrant in almost every state. They were now calling for the complete abolition of alcohol at the federal level. By 1916, many states enacted laws restricting the consumption of alcohol. In 1919, the Eighteenth Amendment was ratified, prohibiting the sale and manufacture of alcohol. It went into effect on January 16, 1920.

The Volstead Act, in addition to the Eighteenth Amendment, was passed in 1919. The act stated that beer, wine, or any other type of alcohol with more than 0.5 percent alcohol was illegal. It also stated that anyone manufacturing or distilling alcohol would be fined or jailed. After this law was passed, there was a significant rise in illegal production and sale of alcohol. Many citizens were unable to reproduce liquors and spirits on their own—and bathtub gin tasted like bath water—so they sought to buy liquor illegally. The illegal sale of alcohol caused organized crime to flourish at a level that simply could not be controlled by local police squads.

In Chicago, one of the most famous gangsters to profit from the illegal sale of alcohol was Al Capone. Some crime bosses would hire "rumrunners" to smuggle whiskey from the Caribbean or Canada. Others would purchase large quantities of homemade distilled liquor from underground moonshine operations. Speakeasies— secret or "underground" bars—sprung up all over the country, allowing people to drink illegally and out of sight from the police.

As soon as the Eighteenth Amendment was passed, organizations formed to repeal it. The temperance movement failed in its promise to bring about an end to the evils of alcohol, and the anti-Prohibition movement gained strength as the 1920s progressed. The stock market crash in 1929 and the beginning of the Great Depression changed people's attitudes toward the Eighteenth Amendment. People needed jobs, and the government needed money. Making alcohol legal again would resuscitate new jobs for citizens and mean additional sales taxes for the government. On December 5, 1933, the Twenty-First Amendment was ratified, repealing the Eighteenth Amendment.

Even with Prohibition—or perhaps because of it—the pub culture of America changed during the 1920s, creating a direct line to the bars that exist today. Pubs and saloons were no longer unsavory places where men engaged in evils of society, and women were allowed in drinking establishments once available only to men.

The Modern American Bar

As the American economy flourished after World War II, Americans continued to focus on the dangers of alcohol abuse. Still, the modern American of the roaring 1920s embraced change in every way: culture, style, social values, and morals. As such, new drinks called "cocktails" became popular. Both men and women attached a new, glamorous image to drinking in public (and even in private). In the 1950s, new technologies and household products led to a growing middle class in America with leisure time for indulging in their favorite pastimes at home. Television and movies on the big screen began presenting liquor, cigarettes, and other products as desirable; Americans appeared stylish if they drank certain brands of drinks and smoked certain brands of cigarettes. Cocktail parties at home became fashionable in the 1950s and 1960s. Casual dining in restaurants that sold cocktails, beer, and wine was becoming more popular. Beer, wine, and spirits were now available for purchase at large grocery stores and liquor stores. A liquor cabinet or bar at home was just like any another piece of furniture in the house. Fixing a drink after coming home from work was also becoming a household practice. Along with the commuter culture of working in the big city and commuting back to the suburbs or to bedroom communities, these trends led to the decline of the popularity of the town bar.

In the early 1970s, 77 percent of men and 60 percent of women were drinkers who frequented bars. But by 1977, those figures began to decline. Furthermore, in the 1970s a law was passed that allowed people to brew beer in their own homes, resulting in the microbrewery culture and the birth of a new industry. Bartenders had to do more than just serve drink to retain customers. Flair bartending became popular in the 1990s as bartenders sought to regain the customers they lost and to entice new ones through the barroom doors.

After this three-decade decline, local bars are once again flourishing. The Internet has revolutionized the way Americans communicate, work, and spend their leisure time. Now that more than one quarter of the working adults in the United States work at home, neighborhood bars are gaining regular customers in increasing numbers.

Niche marketing has also taken a foothold in the bar business, and all types of specialty bars are surfacing, such as sports bars, singles bars, gay bars, wine bars, dive bars, and biker bars. In the twenty-first century, bars continue to hold a solid market share in the economy—there is a future for the drinking establishment yet again.

A Brief History of American Restaurants

Delmonico's Restaurant was the first restaurant in New York City to bring fine dining to America. In 1827, Giovanni and Pietro Delmonico (Italian immigrants and brothers) opened for business, and their restaurant prospered for 100 years. The Delmonico brothers set the standards for fine dining for centuries to come.

Chicago, a bustling center of railroad commerce, was one of the first cities to offer luxury sleeper cars on its trains. The railroads were big business in the nineteenth century, and travelers wanted luxury accommodations as they went west. George Pullman, the creator of the Pullman sleeper car, developed an elegant dining railroad car complete with waiters and chefs. The menus featured fresh, local meat and produce procured along the route of the railroad lines.

In 1893, the Waldorf Hotel (a precursor to the present-day Waldorf Astoria) opened its first luxury dining room, which featured mirrors, lavish furnishings, and superior guest service. Many of its patrons were famous celebrities and wealthy folk of the time. That same year, the self-service restaurant emerged when John Kruger created the cafeteria. It featured virtually no table service, and food was displayed on counters for customers to select for themselves and carry on trays to cashier booths. A flat rate was charged for food. Today, cafeteria-style eating is very common in settings where large numbers of people need to eat in a short period of time—schools, colleges, malls with food courts, and large businesses all have cafeteria-style restaurants. Technological developments have led to better cafeteria cleanliness and easier food dispensation.

By the early twentieth century, the restaurant industry as we know it began to take shape. Americans were traveling by automobile and the need for consistency in quality service and good food at roadside establishments grew evident. The franchise restaurant

INTERVIEW

Changes in the Hospitality Industry

Kate DeCosta,
Corporate Director of Sales, The Newport Experience, Newport, Rhode Island

When did you begin working in the hotel industry?
I got my first hotel job in a 19-room property in Newport, Rhode Island, in 1988, between my junior and senior years in college (at the University of Rhode Island).

Did you receive any sort of formal academic training before you began working in a hotel? If so, what sort? If not, did you worry that not getting a degree might hinder your path to success?
I graduated from college with a bachelor of science, having double majored in political science and finance. I think the finance degree helped in my quick rise in the industry because I had a familiarity with numbers and economics that my colleagues didn't.

What was your first hotel job? What were your responsibilities? How did your career path evolve?
My first job was a front desk clerk. Because it was a small property, this position was more encompassing than the average front desk position. I was responsible for duties ranging from payroll reporting to baking for breakfast. It was actually a management position disguised as a front desk job! I believe that I really learned hospitality while working there. There is much more opportunity to spend time with guests on a small property, and I really learned the needs of travelers/tourists quickly. Since then, I moved with the same company to a start up in Miami's South Beach. They had purchased and were renovating three properties, totaling 145 rooms. It was the beginning of the renaissance of that area and I was fortunate enough to work with a great entrepreneur who had extraordinary vision. Today his property remains an icon in a very fickle market. After Miami, I worked for a corporate flag (Doubletree) and a private club (New York Yacht Club), and am currently in a position with a hospitality company in Newport with annual revenues exceeding $11 million. One of our properties is a 25-room mansion that's been converted into a hotel.

I am corporate director of sales and marketing, and my focus is on catering and event sales with group room bookings being a major piece.

Have any job descriptions changed since you got your start? Have any roles become obsolete?

I think titles remain basically the same, but with an added twist to seem more VIP. We tend to massage words to make titles sound more upscale these days. For instance, the catering manager who handles the dining room is now the "private dining manager." The concierge is now the "personal assistant." The responsibilities are essentially the same, but overall guest satisfaction has never been more important than it is today and the competition in this particular market is fierce. The only roles that may have become obsolete are those that have been replaced by technology. General service remains the same.

Was it common for hotel employees to switch over to restaurant work and vice versa at the beginning of your career? More or less so than today?

In this market, restaurant jobs are always more desirable at the entry level because the compensation is greater. It is always a challenge in the hospitality industry to get servers into management because their pay immediately decreases. Eventually, the benefits associated with management outweigh the instant gratification (cash) of the server position, but not in the beginning. As for crossover, I think it is the same today as when I started my career.

What other sorts of changes have you seen over the course of your career in the hotel industry?

Generally, I've seen the emergence of a genuine concern for customer satisfaction. The old attitude seemed to be "if you don't like it, too bad." Today, more and more companies are featuring feedback programs and the data that is collected is priceless. In this climate, in particular (which really started with the recession of 2008), value-added offers are abundant. Adding a fourth or fifth night for free would have been laughable five years ago, but now it is the norm. Packaging and "togethering," which is the term for nonfamilial groups traveling together, are on the rise and timeshare or "vacation clubs" are also on the rise as more families are demanding cooking facilities in order to save money.

was a concept developed as early as 1925 by Howard Johnson, who expanded his business from a small soda shop into 150 franchises across the United States. Theme restaurants, in which the restaurant's atmosphere was mirrored in its menu, became popular in the 1930s. For example, Victor Bergeron, a bomber pilot during World War II who had spent time in the Polynesian Islands, started a Tiki-themed restaurant in California that blossomed into a worldwide chain. Bergeron may also have invented the Mai Tai cocktail. Diners also became a popular place to eat in the United States during the early 1900s—the first of which was opened by Walter Anderson in Wichita, Kansas. Walt Anderson decided to create a place where customers could be served quick and easy meals, and he later created White Castle, one of the first fast food restaurants in America.

McDonald's is by far the most well-known fast food restaurant in the world today. The founding owners were two brothers, Nick and Maurice (Mac) McDonald. Ray Kroc, a milkshake machine salesman, was fascinated by the idea that the McDonald brothers had franchised eight locations serving French fries, Coca Cola, and milkshakes faster and cheaper than in any diner. In 1954, Kroc received permission to open his own location in Des Plaines, Illinois. In four years, Kroc had grown his business to its 100 millionth hamburger. Kroc built a fast food empire in a short amount of time—all based on the concept of fast service, a tasty burger, and a refreshing milkshake.

In 1954, James McLamore and Dave Edgerton opened the first Burger King in Miami, Florida, and it quickly became a competitor of McDonald's. What made Burger King famous was the concept that customers could have their burger built any way they wanted it. The Burger King burger was also larger—with more beef and bun for the customer. "Have it your way" was Burger King's mantra for success.

While McDonald's is the most recognized brand of fast food, it was not the first. As previously mentioned, Walt Anderson—along with Billy Ingram—opened the first White Castle restaurant in Wichita, Kansas, in 1921. It was a cheap meal—a nickel a burger during the Depression. Anderson and Ingram printed coupons in the newspapers to draw customers. This new and radical concept of advertising in a newspaper by using coupons was a success and the company branched out to open more restaurants by 1936.

By the 1960s, many other fast food chains became part of the American food landscape, meeting the needs of a growing population who literally needed to eat and run. In the 1970s, community dining grew in popularity and began to develop around community-based ideas or projects. Vegetarian restaurants became common. Moosewood Restaurant opened in Ithaca, New York, in 1972, where diners met regularly to share a family-style vegetarian meal. Ethnic restaurants also began to emerge around this time.

Today's restaurants are a product of more than 100 years of American restaurant history. Big, identifiable chains that have full menus and table service are once again popular and can be found all over America. Many neighborhoods and regions have also have a variety local restaurants—including fine dining establishments, fast food restaurants, diners, ethnic restaurants, and vegetarian restaurants.

A Brief History of American Hotels

While the first American inn opened its doors in 1607, the first building in America constructed with the intention of serving as a hotel—the City Hotel in New York City—opened in 1794. With 73 rooms, it was an unusually large property. The City Hotel offered accommodations and meeting rooms, and quickly became the social center of the city. Boston, Baltimore, and Philadelphia followed suit by opening similar establishments, which also quickly became fashionable meeting places.

The Tremont House in Boston opened in 1829. Its claim was first class service, and it boasted 170 rooms, each with its own water pitcher and free soap. There were also single rooms and double rooms with doors that locked—an entirely new concept. Its staff was well trained and they understood that the needs of their guests were of utmost importance. There was also a bellhop who ran messages to and from guests in its rooms.

Between 1830 and 1875, many great hotels were built on the East Coast and in the Midwest. The Grand Pacific, the Palmer House, and the Sherman House opened in Chicago. The Planters opened in St. Louis, while the Paxton was built in Omaha, Nebraska. On the West Coast, the Palace was built in San Francisco during the Gold Rush. One of the most luxurious and expensive hotels of its day, it cost $5 million to build, and opened in 1875 with 800 rooms, covering 2.5 acres in the heart of the city.

In the 1920s and 1930s, many of the great name hotels were built, such as the Waldorf-Astoria, the New York Pennsylvania Hotel, and the Stevens in Chicago (which is now known as the Hilton and Towers). As more expensive hotels rose, so did their room prices. Lodging was no longer affordable for everyone. Americans could now get lodging according to their economic class: luxury hotels were reserved for the rich, leaving less-expensive lodging for the average middle-class citizen.

As Americans began traveling in cars in greater numbers, America saw an increase in roadside hotels and small roadside cabins. The word *motel* was coined from the combination of *motor* and *hotel*. Early motels were usually family-owned affairs, with rooms that resembled cabins. By the 1950s, more travelers demanded better service, bigger rooms, and more comfortable accommodations. Motels offered clean rooms, easy parking, and convenience for salesmen as well as the family on vacation. From 1939 to 1960, over 35,000 motels were built in the United States.

The First Hotel Chains

The hotel industry is filled with ambitious people who start out on the periphery of the lodging industry and work their way up into management, eventually sometimes even owning shares in or purchasing the hotels for which they work. The history of hotel chains is full of such industrious people who worked their way up to become magnates, shaping the industry as we know it today.

In 1927, Willard Marriott, operated a food stand from which he sold root beer and tacos in Washington, D.C. Marriott began to contract food services with businesses (such as large commercial airlines) and even the government (including the Pentagon). While the name Marriott is today synonymous with large hotel conglomerates, Marriott did not become an extensive hotel chain until the 1980s. During the 1960s, Will Marriott dealt only in food contracts, and began to provide food to public schools under the name Hot Shoppes. Hot Shoppes purchased the Howard Johnson restaurants, renaming the company Marriott. Marriott also bought two theme parks in the 1980s and continues to expand overseas today, buying into markets such as vacation clubs and senior-living condos. Its corporate headquarters still remains in Washington, D.C.

Conrad Hilton founded Hilton Hotels in 1919. The first hotel he opened was in Texas, his native state. Hilton Hotels were built and designed with the intention of dedicating as much space as possible to the comfort of their guests—Hilton wanted his guests to head straight to the Hilton Hotel in any city to which they traveled. Business travel was a focal point for Hilton from the beginning of his company. In 1954, he bought the Statler hotel company—the largest real estate transaction of its time. Today, Hilton Hotels has expanded into international markets, and has opened a new line of luxury hotels named Conrad Hotels and Resorts, which can be found in vacation destinations in countries such as Puerto Rico, Turkey, and the Maldives. The corporate headquarters are in Cisco, Texas.

The Ritz-Carlton Hotel opened in Boston in 1927. It was to be a world-class hotel offering luxury accommodations to its guests. Dress codes were required for guests and women were restricted in the restaurants until the 1970s. The Ritz-Carlton designed and made its own furniture and hired its own printmakers for hanging pictures. Privacy of guests was strictly adhered to. The Ritz-Carlton continues to be an icon of sterling standards in the hospitality industry. The hotel chain has grown internationally and today has hotels in such faraway places as Qatar, Singapore, and Russia. The company is headquartered in Bethesda, Maryland.

On the Cutting Edge

Automatic Reservation

Hilton Reservations Worldwide (HRW) was the original central reservations center implemented in the hotel industry. Since its introduction, HRW has had an tremendous impact on the growth of Hilton Hotels Corporation and Hilton International Corporation by centralizing the booking process for all Hilton hotels at sophisticated call centers (and Web sites) that maximize the number of reservations while simultaneously minimizing the required number of employees for the task.

The Best Western Hotel chain grew from a network of family-owned hotels and roadside motels that formed the Best Western Hotels in 1946. These hotels contract with the main entity Best Western, but are allowed to carry their own identities with the name "Best Western" attached to them. The company is headquartered in Phoenix.

Las Vegas was home to a major boom in the hotel industry in the early 1900s. As a railroad stop along the way to California in the 1890s, it soon gave life to saloons, stores, and small boarding houses for travelers en route to California. Gambling was a popular pastime at the start of the town, and when it was legalized tax revenue from gambling was used to fund public schools. In the 1940s, strip hotel construction was booming and the Pink Flamingo Hotel was constructed to house a hotel and casino. Today, the Flamingo Resort—the oldest resort on the strip operating today—houses a 77,000 foot casino, a garden chapel, and a flamingo wildlife habitat with live penguins and flamingos in addition to many other exotic birds and fish.

Although large hotel chains dominated the lodging market, there remained room in the hotel market other big players. For example, Stephen Alan Wynn is land developer who was interested in the casinos of Las Vegas. He helped develop and open the Mirage, a lavish casino with attractions including an indoor forest and a working volcano, and he has since helped to open two other major casino resorts. His most recent endeavor was the opening of Wynn Macau in 2008.

A Brief Chronology

Circa 960 B.C.E.: Chinese restaurants are already part of Chinese culture in Kaifeng, China.

50 B.C.E.: Romans brew beer and produce wine. They carry their techniques with them throughout the regions they conquer all the way to Northern Europe. Inns are established along the Roman Long Road for travelers.

500–1000 A.D.: European monasteries and convents are bodes of hospitality for travelers who are treated to carefully brewed beer and simple foods.

Mid to late fourteenth century: Taverns are typical stopping points along the routes of travel in Europe. Lodging and food is available. Live entertainment is common.

1688: Coffeehouses become popular among captains of industry who do their business in many of these houses throughout Europe.

1762: Fraunces' Tavern opens on Pearl and Broad streets in New York City, serving food and beer. Although delivery of food to customers was previously unheard of, the tavern frequently sends meals to George Washington when he stays in town. Fraunces' Tavern becomes a famous site as the seeds of the American Revolution are sown there.

1765: A Paris tavern-keeper cooks and serves a soup in his tavern that is made of sheep's fat and calls it a *restaurant* (translation: a "restorative"). He is sued by the French food guilds for selling food in his tavern. He wins the lawsuit and his business begins to boom. The concept of a restaurant is born.

1794: The City Hotel opens for business in New York City. It is the country's first hotel.

1827: Delmonico's restaurant opens in New York City. It offers fine dining to its customers, who are mainly New York City's elite. Delmonico's is considered the standard for luxury dining for over 100 years.

1829: The Tremont Hotel opens in Boston. It is considered the first luxury hotel.

1868: Commercial brewing and distilling of beer and alcohol begins in the United States. Railroad distribution is an important part of the industry. George Pullman designs and builds the first dining car on the railroad complete with a butler and wait staff.

1875: The Palace hotel opens in San Francisco. It is a large, lavish hotel built on 2.5 acres.

1893: The Waldorf Hotel (a precursor to the present-day Waldorf-Astoria) opens with a luxury dining room. The dining room is considered to be a fine dining restaurant on its own, given its reputation for elegant service, its lavish surroundings, and elite clientele.

1895: The Temperance Movement gains a foothold in American society. The Anti-Saloon League is founded. Carrie Nation becomes famous for wrecking saloons and bars.

1898: John Kruger opens a self-service restaurant which he names "cafeteria" at the World's Columbian Exposition in Chicago.

1916: The first diner opens in Wichita, Kansas. Walt Anderson names his diner White Castle and serves a meal of hamburger and fries for ten cents. White Castle is the forefather to the fast food restaurant.

1919: Prohibition begins when Congress passes the Eighteenth Amendment and the Volstead Act that bans the production or sale of any alcoholic beverage. Criminal gangs become wealthy overnight from the sale of illegal alcohol. Speakeasies become popular and flourish. Conrad Hilton opens the first Hilton hotel in Texas.

1925: Howard Johnson creates the first franchise restaurant. Johnson proceeds to opens 150 more franchises on the East Coast.

1927: A Ritz-Carlton opens in Boston. This luxury hotel requires a dress code for its guests.

1933: The Twenty-First Amendment repeals Prohibition. American breweries and other distilleries are in decline. Foreign breweries and distilleries gain a foothold in the market.

1934: The Rainbow Room opens in New York City. It is a fancy supper club for elite New Yorkers.

1936: Victor Bergeron opens the Tiki Room. It is the first theme restaurant in America.

1940: The Pink Flamingo Hotel and Casino is opened in Las Vegas. This is the first of many hotel and gambling casinos to be opened in Las Vegas.

1948: Richard and Maurice McDonald open McDonald's Restaurant.

1950: Many motels open up along the major highways of America to provide affordable lodging for travelers.

1954: Ray Kroc purchases a McDonald's restaurant, revolutionizing the fast food industry as he creates the McDonald's empire.

1972: Americans are becoming socially conscious about their health and well-being and the environment. Restaurants are now conceived based on alternative lifestyles and ideologies. Restaurants that are organic, vegetarian, communal, and slow food-based become more popular.

1978: President Jimmy Carter signs a bill legalizing the brewing of homemade beer, giving the micro-brewery industry a boost.

2000s: Haute Cuisine restaurants that feature ethnic fusion dining become popular. Themed bars become popular and neighborhood bars make a comeback.

2008: Casino Resorts are built with grander-than-ever accommodations, offering increasingly elegant service and whimsical features.

Chapter 2

State of the Industry

The hospitality industry is continuously evolving. Like many industries, it weathers the economy during downturns and prospers during good times. Investments in future trends will launch the industry into another decade of profitability—provided managers and owners stay focused on the needs and wants of their customers. The preparation of responsible leaders within the industry is also critical to the industry's success. As American cuisine has gained respect the world over, and American hotels continue to set the global standard, chefs, hoteliers, designers, and the entire range of service people involved in the industry need to be trained to be creative, innovative, and, above-all *service-oriented*.

This chapter examines three sub-industries under the umbrella of the hospitality industry: hotels and lodging, restaurants, and gaming. These three sectors rely on several factors to be profit-making entities: a reliable customer base, capital, and a healthy economy. Using these profit-making factors as a lens, this chapter examines trends, market share, the major players in each sector, the major trade events for each sector, legal issues, and wages and salaries for jobs in lodging, restaurants and casinos.

Lodging Industry Overview

The lodging sector of the hospitality industry comprises hotels, motels, bed-and-breakfasts, hostels, campgrounds, and other places where a guest can stay overnight. Well-known brand names like

Econo-Lodge, Super 8, and Motel 6 are considered budget accommodations. Mid-priced lodgings are hotels such as Sheraton and Marriott, while high-end luxury hotels include the W Hotels and the Ritz-Carlton.

The lodging industry is capital-intensive, meaning it requires large investments of revenue to create a good product. Therefore, the lodging industry must turn to heavy marketing by using tools like slogans, logos, designs, and media exposure to attract a loyal customer population. Plant and facility maintenance also greatly impacts how well a hotel is able to advertise itself. Room amenities and clean facilities are the two major marketing foci in the hotel industry. However, in an effort to draw more customers, hotels are turning to the business segment of the market by offering services such as conference or meeting rooms, office services, and Internet access.

Industry metrics track and report profits by retail sales, occupancy rates, average daily room prices (ADR), and revenue per available room (RevPAR). RevPAR is calculated by multiplying a hotel's occupancy rate by its average daily room rate. Computer systems that assist in the reservation of airline tickets, rental cars, hotel rooms, and tours are called computer reservation systems (CRS) or global distribution systems (GDS). They have changed how the hospitality industry operates, and they continue to impact how customers are served. Large hotel chains have their own computer systems that enable them to track guest reservations, provide guest services, and view room charges.

The lodging sector of the industry serves both vacationers and business travelers. Revenues were $103 billion in 2002 and increased to $140.6 billion by 2008, according to the Hotel Operating Statistics Study (HOST). The average daily rate (or the average cost of a room) reached a record high of $106.55 in 2008, a 0.9 percent increase from 2007.

According to Hoover's, a Web site that publishes business reports, there are 30,000 lodging companies operating in 50,000 locations in the United States with a combined annual revenue of more than $90 billion. Most hotels are part of a chain, with large U.S. companies holding 45 percent of total market share. Major players include Marriot International, Carlson Hotels, Hilton Hotels, and Starwood Hotels and Resorts. In 2009, the average hotel will earn roughly $7 million in annual revenue and will employ about 100 people.

Hoover's reports that basic hotel operations revenue comes from room fees (70 percent of industry revenue), sale of food (15 percent of revenue) and liquor (5 percent of revenue), and miscellaneous merchandise. Most hotels offer housekeeping, maintenance, business services, event hosting, and resort service (such as tennis, swimming pools, and fitness centers) in addition to sleeping accommodations.

Lodging Employment, Wages, and Salaries

The hospitality industry is not one in which an individual can expect to get rich quickly. That said, management positions in big hotel and lodging chains do pay well, and most employees can expect a comfortable living.

According to the Bureau of Labor and Statistics, the industry will have seen a 17 percent increase in jobs by 2014. Twenty-one percent of current wage earners are between the ages of 16 and 19. Because of the industry's growth rate and the use of a young workforce, it is a priority of the industry to find good employees. The number of young workers creates the erroneous impression that only low-wage, entry-level jobs are available in the industry. On the contrary: wages can have a 5 percent to 10 percent variance depending on actual job duties, years of experience, location, and type of lodging.

The Hospitality Career Network has a vast listing of the management jobs in the lodging industry. In 2009, the nationwide salary for general managers ranged from $85,616 to $129,368, with banquet managers earning from $42,436 to $65,740, depending on the size of the hotel. A bookkeeper earns as much as $44,000 per year.

According to Payscale.com, the median hourly rate for a concierge is $10.10 to $15, while a desk clerk's pay might range from $7 to $15 per hour, and a shift manager might earn anywhere from $8.32 to

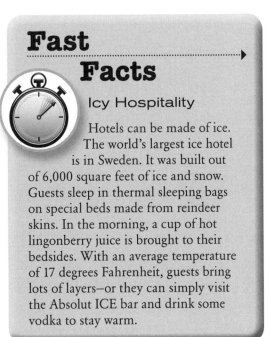

Fast Facts

Icy Hospitality

Hotels can be made of ice. The world's largest ice hotel is in Sweden. It was built out of 6,000 square feet of ice and snow. Guests sleep in thermal sleeping bags on special beds made from reindeer skins. In the morning, a cup of hot lingonberry juice is brought to their bedsides. With an average temperature of 17 degrees Fahrenheit, guests bring lots of layers—or they can simply visit the Absolut ICE bar and drink some vodka to stay warm.

$17.69 hour. Administrative assistants generally earn $13 per hour, and sales coordinators about $13.50 per hour.

Lodging Industry Trends

From technological developments to the rise of niche hotels and lifestyle branding, the lodging industry is host to many burgeoning business trends.

The Internet

The Internet has changed the nature of the hospitality industry. Consumers can now compare prices and services with ease. Travel agents used to be invaluable—they would handle a trip for a customer by calling hotels, booking tickets, and making reservations. The Internet has rendered the travel agent obsolete, in many respects. Consumers can research destinations, compare prices, and visit hotel and entertainment Web sites that provide most, if not all, of the information they need. Web sites such as Expedia, Orbitz, Travelocity, and Cendant allow customers access to online price comparisons. According to Hoover's, 12 percent of lodging reservations are now made online, and that number is sure to grow in coming years. According to industry experts, the Internet has increased the number of rooms occupied per night, but decreased revenue per room, as the ease of Internet comparison shopping and Internet-only promos have increased competition among hospitality providers.

Today's hotels are in fierce competition with each other because of their savvy customer base. Consequently, customer services must now be sterling. Desk clerks, tour guides, and other folks on the front lines must be friendly, positive, and articulate at all times. And while excellent service is a great draw for guests, word of mouth still remains the best kind of advertisement.

Niche Hotels

One way that hotels have stayed competitive is by entering niche markets. In the hospitality industry, niche markets are specialty services—gaming resorts, golf resorts, shopping excursions, and eco-tourism. Destination vacations and tours of all kinds are now big business. Tours have exploded as a market—tours to Jerusalem;

tours catering to single women, gay men, or fans of Broadway shows; ski and snowboard tours, snorkeling/deep sea diving tours, and adventure travel.

Some large companies have a firm grasp on niche markets. Along with newly themed concepts, many hotels now offer extreme perks in order to attract guests. Walt Disney World is a big player in the family vacation market. Club Med offers vacations for families, too, as well as for couples. Other big players are Sandals and Fairfield Resorts. Hotel Sax in Chicago is themed for jazz music lovers. Formerly known as the House of Blues Hotel, Hotel Sax is a luxurious hotel that features snakeskin wingback chairs, paisley-embossed leather headboards, and painted silhouettes of phantom chandeliers in all of its 353 rooms. The service people are extremely helpful and very enthusiastic about their work. The Sax encourages guests to mingle and socialize in areas throughout the hotel, including its lounge, Crimson. The House of Blues club adjacent to the hotel hosts performances at all hours of the day and night. Hotel Sax serves as a temporary home to people in the music business, including roadies and managers who create a high-energy atmosphere. For guests only, there is a state-of-the-art technology lounge stocked with laptops, video games like Guitar Hero, downloadable music, movies, and HDTV screens (which are wired together so that Xbox players can play each other from across the room).

Eco-Friendly Hotels

Using environmentally friendly and allergy-free products, eco-friendly hotels are marketed to environmentally-conscious customers. Energy-efficient lighting, eco-smart dispensers, green key card systems, eco-friendly and recyclable food and beverage ware, clean-air environmental products, and bio-degradable soap, shampoos, and oils are just some of the features and offerings at eco-friendly hotels. For example, California's Solage Calistoga has an eco-luxe theme for its guests who are environmentally conscious but still seeking stylish accommodations. The 89-room resort consists of stand-alone studios and is surrounded by scrubby young vegetation. Guests can bicycle to morning yoga and enjoy fruit and granola at the open-air Solbar restaurant. The lounge by the pool is lined with sago palms. The guesthouses, painted in cooling taupe and sage tones, have huge slate-floor bathrooms and spare, dark-wood furniture. Complimentary bicycles are available for guest use. Shaded patios allow for guest privacy. The service is helpful and when guests check in they are treated to welcoming cupcakes and full-sized coffeepots.

In an increasingly environmentally conscious world, hotels like Solage Calistoga, which are on the eco-friendly cutting edge, will enjoy an ever-increasing market share, and employees with an understanding of this fast-growing employment sector will likely find themselves in ever-increasing demand.

Branding

Hoover's has reported that strong branding will be more important than most other market trends in the years to come. Brand name hotels are growing globally, and strong branding is necessary to drive online direct bookings, to differentiate and avoid commoditization, and to provide leverage against online intermediaries. To further enhance the bond and brand value, significant investments will be made in brand/franchisee portals, which will enhance and streamline both processes and information delivery.

Other Trends: Self Service, Blogs for Guests, and Mobile Technology

One recent trend in particular that will continue to grow is self-service. Common use self-service (CUSS) will streamline travel and lodging. For example, hotels are working with airlines to enable guests to print their boarding passes at hotels during check-out—a tremendous convenience for the passenger/guest.

Another major trend is blogs created by and for hotel guests. Blogs can add to the word-of-mouth business on which many hospitality businesses rely. Blogs also provide hotels with a defensive strategy by enabling them to control reviews, recommendations, and complaints. An interactive communication forum enables a relationship between the hotel and the customer beyond the customer's actual stay at the hotel.

Mobile technology will also help to increase revenue. According to a hospitality industry report, over 70 percent of U.S. households have at least one cell phone subscriber. Almost 85 percent of those cell phones are Web enabled, and nearly all of them are text enabled. While not yet at the level it will eventually attain, marketing via mobile technology will greatly help the hospitality industry to quickly disseminate promotional information about room deals, upcoming events, and room availability.

Lodging's Major Players

Fortune magazine conducts a thorough and comprehensive employee survey of hundreds of companies all over to world to determine which 100 companies are the best to work for. It turns out that, according to *Fortune*, some of the top companies to work for include the major players in the hospitality industry.

Marriott International is ranked 78th on the *Fortune* list. In 2007, Marriott International's revenue was nearly $13 billion. As of 2009, the hotel chain employed roughly 125,000 people and has shown 2 percent job growth per year despite a downturn in the economy. Marriott International offers great benefits to its employees including waived health insurance co-pays, onsite childcare, job sharing, compressed workweeks, and telecommuting. Sixty-one percent of the employee population belong to a minority group and 55 percent of employees are women, a strong indicator of the company's diversity. Salaried jobs include sales manager positions that pay approximately $63,000, to executive managers who may earn $125,000. Marriott has a large presence in the New York market and employs over 4,000 people in that area. Marriott International has taken steps to remain a competitive force in the lodging sector by cutting spending in every department.

Four Seasons Hotels ranked 92nd on the *Fortune* list. Four Seasons Hotels employs about 13,000 people in the United States. Salaried jobs include food and beverage manager, which can pay as much as $52,000. Four Seasons is expected to have four percent job growth in 2009. The company offer benefits such as job sharing, compressed workweeks, and telecommuting. Employees also enjoy perks, such as staying for free at any Four Seasons lodging for up to three nights a year and 50 percent off food service. It has a diverse workforce with 60 percent of employees being minority and 45 percent being women. Four Seasons has a large presence on the East Coast and employs most of its workforce in that region.

Another major player is Carlson Companies, which runs hotels such as the Radisson Hotels, Park Plaza Hotels, and Regent Hotels and Resorts. Carlson Companies was ranked 87th in the top 200 hotel companies of 2009 by the Human Rights Campaign and was recognized as one of the top ranking companies to hire a diverse workforce. Carlson offers generous health care benefits, transgender benefits, and their employee population is diverse. Senior managers can earn as much as $60,000. According to *Forbes* magazine, Carlson companies earned $4.3 billion in revenue in 2007. The company employs 55,000 people worldwide.

Harrah's Entertainment is one of the largest gaming establishments in the casino industry. In 2008, Harrah's Entertainment was ranked 236th out of the top 1,000 companies by *Fortune* and was ranked in the top 200 hotel companies by *Forbes*. Harrah's is one of the world's largest casino businesses located in Las Vegas, employing 87,000 people. The entertainment group earned $10 billion in revenue in 2007.

Everyone Knows

House Rules

In hotels and restaurants, *back of house* refers to tasks performed outside the view of guests, while *front of house* indicates those involving direct customer interaction.

Wynn Resorts was ranked 731st in 2008 as one of the 1,000 best companies to work for in the hotel industry by *Forbes*, and was ranked 691st in 2009 by Fortune's equivalent list. Wynn Resorts is based in two locations: Las Vegas and Macau. Wynn Resorts offers full health benefits, including bereavement leave, employee assistance programs, and FMLA leave. Wynn Resorts saw a decline in revenue in 2009 but the company avoided layoffs by instituting pay cuts, cutting back on work hours, and reducing bonuses. Wynn's revenue for 2008 was $2.9 billion.

Forbes 200 lists Global Hyatt as the 93rd largest company in 2007 in the United States. Hyatt owns 365 hotels and resorts around the world and earned $4 billion in revenues in 2007. Hyatt Hotels employs 90,000 worldwide. Hyatt did cut some jobs in 2009, but extended health care benefits for workers who were let go.

Hilton Hotels is considered a leader in the hospitality industry. The company's revenue for 2007 was approximately $8 billion. Hilton has very recognizable hotels in every major city in the United States. Hilton brands include Doubletree, Embassy Suites, and Hampton and includes the prestigious Waldorf-Astoria. Hilton Hotels has a workforce of 130,000 employees worldwide who work for 3,300 hotels. Employee benefits include healthcare, job security, pensions, and wage increases.

Restaurant Industry Overview

The restaurant industry is made up of high, mid-tier, and lower-tier restaurants. Within each of those levels, there are many different types of restaurants, ranging from casual to full-service and fine dining. Customers have many choices about what time of dining establishment they choose, whether they are seeking American or European or Latin American food, fast food, or a Michelin-rated dining room.

According to the National Restaurant Association, restaurant sales are forecasted to grow by 2.5 percent in 2009, with industry sales exceeding $1.5 trillion. Every additional million dollars in the restaurant industry generates 33 new jobs for the U.S. economy. Ninety-one percent of the restaurants in the United States are considered small businesses because they employ 50 or fewer people. In total, the industry employs 13 million people—9 percent of the domestic workforce—and expects to add 1.8 million jobs by 2019. One quarter of U.S. restaurants are owned by women, Asians own 15 percent of restaurants, 8 percent are owned by Hispanics, and 4 percent are African-American owned. Restaurant sales for a single day often total $1.5 billion in the United States.

Restaurant Employment, Wages, and Salaries

The average wages in 2008 for back-of-house restaurant jobs are as follows: executive chefs earned an average of $85,179, sous chefs earned roughly $44,205, while line cooks earned an average of $12.90 per hour.

According to the Bureau of Labor Statistics, waiters earned an average hourly wage of $9.41. The annual mean salary for waiters was $19,580. Similarly, the average wage for bartenders was $20,460. Waiters and bartenders rely heavily on tips in order to make a living wage. Bussers and barbacks earned an average wage of $8.72 per hour. Waiters and bartenders share a portion of their tips with bussers and barbacks, depending on the policy of the bar or restaurant where they work. Dishwashers earned an average of $8.91 per hour. Wages vary depending on the region of the country, with large cities and more populated areas showing higher wages. Upscale bars, restaurants, hotels, and country clubs pay their workers wages that are 5 to 10 percent higher than the mean wage.

Restaurant Industry Trends

Restaurant trends are driven by what is new and hot in the food and beverage market, what exciting new recipes are bubbling to the top, and how innovatively they are prepared. Restaurants are constantly tackling these new tastes by changing their menus to meet their customers' ever-evolving demands. A restaurant's menu determines what kind of eatery it is; for example, an establishment that serves sushi is a Japanese restaurant, one that serves Mexican fare is a Mexican restaurant, and so on. If a Mexican restaurant decides to add sushi to its menu, it becomes a Mexican/Japanese fusion restaurant.

According to the U.S. Industry Report by Ibisworld.com, industry trends show that consumer tastes have shifted over time toward a preference for Middle Eastern, Mexican, Japanese, Thai, Caribbean, and Italian food. Another big shift in restaurants is the increase in healthy and/or low calorie offerings. These, along with other major industry trends, are discussed below.

Local Produce and Artisan Products

In a 2008 survey of 1,600 chefs, the American Culinary Federation asked its members to rate 208 individual food and beverage items, preparation methods, and culinary themes according to categories such as "hot trend," "yesterday's news," or "perennial favorite." The use of locally grown produce was rated as the number-one trend, as many of today's consumers want farm-fresh fruit and vegetables that have seen little transportation. Using locally grown and raised items shows support for local communities and businesses.

Foods and beverages produced by small, artisan businesses also hold appeal. *Artisan* refers to food that is made by hand and sold in small batches. Cheeses, breads, and meats sold by family-owned farms are part of the artisan food movement. Animal welfare (meaning how animals are treated and slaughtered) has become important to the food consumer as well. Grain-fed and free-range pigs, cattle, and chickens allow the consumer to eat more healthful products.

Healthy Menus

The top food trends expected to increase in popularity (according to the NDP Group, a major marketing research company) involve healthy eating. Most restaurants now carry diet and/or low-calorie items, and many restaurants now offer customers the opportunity to opt out of sides or choose healthier ones based on their eating habits and diets. In the 2008 American Culinary Federation survey, the creation of healthy kids' meals was also a top trend. Kids' side dishes that include vegetables and fruit were particularly hot.

Going Green

As the culinary arts continue to grow in the United States, consumers are learning more about the food they are eating. Using local and sustainable ingredients is one new trend that is a result of this increasing consumer education. "Going green," as within the hotel industry, is another. Going green will affect cooking methods, the use of energy sources, and the hunt for new local food sources. Restaurant kitchens of the future will become increasingly environmentally friendly, using eco-friendly equipment and practices while finding ways to save money through sustainable practices.

Slow Food Movement

Another new trend is the slow food movement, which is related to trends mentioned above. The slow food movement stands in stark contrast to fast food culture. The focus of the slow food movement is on producing good food using environmentally friendly methods, to be sold at a fair price. The slow food movement even has its own organization—founded in the late 1990s, Slow Food USA disseminates information and host discussions for its members and interested people wishing to participate in discussions about promoting the slow food movement. The restaurant industry has taken notice of this new eating philosophy and is responding to it on menus.

Beverage Pairings

Various types of alcohol will also feature greatly on future menus, both as cooking ingredients and on drink menus. Micro-distilled liquor, culinary cocktails—which are created to complement specific foods and dishes—and organic wine top the list of new trends in alcohol. Non-alcoholic beverages that have gained popularity include specialty iced teas, organic coffees, and flavored or enhanced water.

On the Cutting Edge

Mix It Up

"As Americans are growing more and more interested in the culinary arts and the 'foodie' movement, that interest and sophistication is also extending to alcohol and cocktails," claims Dawn Sweeney, President and CEO of the National Restaurant Association. Given the general American fascination with all things new and hip, it behooves anyone working in the bar/restaurant business to be aware of the latest cocktails trends and, when appropriate, incorporate these developments into their own menus.

Alcohol has always been considered a key part to the dining experience. The National Restaurant Association conducted a survey that showed which alcohol trends will be the hottest on restaurant menus in 2009. In addition to micro-distilled/artisan liquor, culinary cocktails, and organic wine, also high on the list were food-alcohol pairings, craft beer, organic cocktails, muddled cocktails, and wine or beer flights. Craft, or specialty, beer is traditional beer that is distilled by small, independent breweries known as micro-breweries. Specialty beers feature ingredients not typically found in mass-produced beer, and are brewed using careful and unique techniques.

A mixologist is a professional who studies the careful mixing of drinks and helps further the field of bartending. His or her profession extends far beyond simply pouring a beer and taking drink orders. A mixologist has been referred to as both a cocktail historian and trendsetter. Unlike mixologists, bartenders tend to pour drinks that are already well known and popular with his or her customers.

Pairing cocktails and wines is all about enhancing the flavor of food. Today's chefs need to know as much as mixologists in order to pair wine and cocktails with the dishes they are serving. In the coming years, chefs will pair many food trends with specialty beers, organic cocktails, and signature drinks. American diners have also become savvy wine drinkers and are always on the lookout for inexpensive wines to complement their dinner choices.

The National Restaurant Association's survey also found that the culinary cocktail is an emerging concept that will become more visible on restaurant menus beginning in 2009. Professional bartenders now have to think of beverage-making much like chefs conceive their recipes. Signature drinks are quickly becoming the culinary cocktail of choice. These cocktails are made using a wider variety of ingredients, more precise mixing techniques, and better-tasting ingredients from the kitchen itself. Signature cocktails are flavored to complement specific dishes on the menu. Items such as basil, bitters, mint, lychee fruit, and edible flowers are all used in culinary cocktails.

Ethnic Restaurants on the Rise, Pricey Restaurants on the Decline

Still more trends that are emerging in the restaurant industry, according to Starchefs.com, include beer sommeliers, upscale noodle bars, and upscale ethnic restaurants. Also, while pricey food, wines, and cocktails are trending downward, prix fixe lunch and dinner menus are expected to become increasingly popular. Ethnic dining, including Spanish, Korean, and other Asian cuisines, is taking the restaurant market by storm. Also, simple American foods with a gourmet twist are now in vogue, such as the gourmet hotdog paired with pommes frites (French fries).

Casual Dining Is In

Casual dining is another current trend. American diners now prefer less-formal service over coat and tie dress, white-gloved waiters, and tableside flambeaus. Chefs are defining how consumers will enjoy their cooking by designing a more casual atmosphere for service and presentation of their food. The old-style, European way of dining no longer plays a role in how American chefs wish to present their cuisine. T-shirts and jeans have even become standard wear for servers in restaurants and bars. Some bars and restaurants in larger cities have taken casual dining and drinking to a different level—they are literally set up like rooms from home, complete with beds, couches, and living room tables.

Communal Dining

Communal dining is still another trend that is quickly taking hold. According to the *Seattle Times*, communal dining is the practice of inviting customers who do not know each other to sit together at large tables to share a meal at the same time. Communal dining is often combined with a prix fixe or family-style meal. The serving time for the meal is set at a discreet hour and others are not allowed to join the meal once it has begun. Communal dining is quickly taking hold as a trend because people enjoy the communal experience, especially those who live in more isolated regions, such as within fenced and gated communities.

Presentation of Food

Presentation of food is another trend that is seeing some extremism. While the plating of dishes has always been a restaurant standard, some restaurants now serve meat, poultry, and fish on beds of "sand" (Panko bread crumbs or coconut), on "seashells" (white pasta), on edible flowers, and on the sea (broth made of clams, mussels and oyster juice). Less ostentatious presentations include dishes served on lily pads, evergreen leaves, and inside banana leaf wraps. All of these presentation methods claim to preserve the aroma and taste of the dish.

Why are today's chefs creating such culinary adventures for their diners? Because their customers are demanding it! According to Starchefs.com, chefs today believe their average diner has a sophisticated palate and is aware of seasonal ingredients and artisan foods and producers within their local regions. They also know that 20 percent of diners want to eat unusual food, prepared in unusual ways. And 25 percent want their eating experience to be one of convenience—delicious but also serviced quickly.

The Major Players—Restaurants

While each city or region has its influential restaurants, on a national scale the major players in the industry are companies that own large chain restaurants with somewhat similar menus, prices, and casual family-style dining styles. For this reason, this section focuses on the three major players in the casual dining sector.

Darden Restaurants owns and operates full service restaurants in the United States and Canada. It is the largest casual dining competitor in the market. Its brands include LongHorn Steakhouse, Bahama Breeze, Red Lobster, The Capital Grille, Olive Garden and Seasons

52. Darden employs about 180,000 people and is expected to earn $7.12 billion in revenue in 2009.

Brinker International, Inc., owns and operates major chain restaurants such as Chili's, Romano's Macaroni Grill, and Maggiano's Little Italy. It comprises 1,900 restaurants all over the world. Brinker International is the second largest restaurant competitor in the market. Brinker International earned $4.3 billion in 2007 and employs over 113,000 employees worldwide.

DineEquity Inc. operates and owns the Applebee and International House of Pancakes (IHOP) restaurants. There are 1,900 Applebee's and 1,300 IHOPs nationwide. The company revamped their restaurants and made them franchises. DineEquity earned $108 million in revenue in 2007.

Casino Industry Overview

Casinos make up a subset of the hospitality industry—one that, in 2008, employed over 375,000 people according to the American Gaming Association. For this reason, casinos are treated in their own subsection in this chapter. Casinos are also one of the fastest growing sections within the hospitality industry: Casino employment increased from 198,657 people in 1990 to 357, 314 people in 2008— an 80 percent increase. Employees earned $14.1 billion in wages in 2008, and in 2007 the industry grossed $92.27 billion. Gambling is an industry that is controlled by 20 major companies who earn 60 percent of the revenue in the business. Gambling is driven by consumer tastes as well as the state of the economy. Casinos tend to have positive impacts on communities because they bring jobs to their hometowns as well as to other sectors of the hospitality industry, including hotels and restaurants. Areas that have casinos tend to have higher hotel and restaurant revenue than non-casino communities. Casinos take in about 60 percent of revenue, restaurants take in about 15 percent in revenue, and hotels get about 10 percent of the revenue when gambling is the main attraction in a community.

Four large casino operations, which are discussed below, are considered the major players in the industry. They receive 70 percent of the revenue earned in the industry. While new government regulations and slow economies seem to threaten the viability of the industry at times, new technology and innovative ideas carry the industry through rough seas.

Casino Wages and Salaries

The most popular jobs in the gaming industry are gaming cage worker, gaming dealer, and gaming manager.

Gaming cage workers work the cashier stalls in casinos. They sell chips or tokens to gamblers, collect chips to be cashed in, perform credit checks and credit references, and make sure paperwork is handled for casino play. They also act as depositories for monies collected from gaming dealers. According to the Bureau of Labor Statistics (BLS), cage work is expected to increase by 11 percent by 2016. Cage workers earn an average of $11.13 per hour, the median 50 percent made between $9.49 and $13.00 per hour, and the top 10 percent made $15.92 per hour.

A gaming dealer deals cards at the card tables, compares the house hands to the players' hands, works the table games, and collects chips from players. According to the BLS, in 2009 about 10 percent of gaming dealers made $15.00 per hour while the median wage was $7.84 per hour. Gaming dealers make a lot of tips from "tokes" (or tokens given as tips).

Gaming managers oversee the operation of the card and game tables on the casino floor. They are there to ensure that customers are enjoying their time at the casino. They also look out for anyone who may be cheating or stealing from the casino. Gaming managers ensure that the casino floor is clean and well maintained. According to the BLS, gaming managers earned about $62,000 per year in 2009 and gaming management will see a 25 percent increase in jobs in the coming years. Most jobs will be found in Las Vegas, Atlantic City, and in California.

Casino Industry Trends

Gambling is no longer considered a despicable form of entertainment to be carried out in seedy saloons. Casinos are opening in many states as laws are loosened to legalize gambling. As more casinos are opened, they are using cutting edge technology, joint ventures, and expanding business ventures to become large profit-making centers.

According to Reuters, joint ventures are a quickly growing trend in the casino industry. Some casinos are signing joint ventures with parts of the government in order to get access to the large amounts of capital needed to run casinos.

Gaming technology is also seeing improvement, especially in slot machines. Gamers will soon be able to pause their slot machines, returning later to résumé their play. Card-shuffling devices have been added to card tables to allow for quicker shuffling of cards and a reduction of card counting. Studies show that cards shuffled by continuous shuffling machines can make a player play as many as 20 percent more hands per hour, thus potentially increasing revenue for the casino.

"Racinos" offer casino gambling with greyhound or horseracing as combined entertainment. According to NPR News, in 2008 racinos created billions of dollars in revenue. States view racinos as good business ventures as they generate much need tax revenue. Racinos have also brought a revival to horse and greyhound racing, which was in decline as a form of entertainment.

Online gambling is the most-noticed new trend in the industry. Major casino companies are supporting online gambling and lobbying for its legalization. According to American Gaming Association CEO Frank Fahrenkopf, online gaming will become a major focal point for the government in the coming years. He hopes that Congress will push for the legalization of Internet gaming and will find ways to both tax and regulate it. Many companies see online gambling as a way to boost their profit margins in a slow economy. Its potential has yet to be realized in terms of a percentage of how much revenue can be earned. Today the United States is the third largest online gambling market in the world.

Casino Major Players

Harrah's Entertainment is the largest casino operation in the world. Its brand names include Harrah's, Caesar's, Horseshoe, and Rio. Harrah's owns casinos all over the world and has exclusive rights to the World Series of Poker, which is a huge moneymaker for the company. Harrah's Entertainment has been able to grow into a very successful operation because it stands behind certain service promises to its customers: superior products, excellent service, and operations that run smoothly. Harrah's is a true leader in providing new gaming technology to customers.

MGM Mirage operates casinos throughout the Midwest, the Northeast, and abroad. In total, MGM owns 17 casinos and is considered one of the industry's leaders in diversity initiatives. MGM Mirage supports responsible gaming and has helped to institute the

Code of Conduct for Responsible Gaming, which was adopted by the American Gaming Association. MGM offers its employees health-care coverage, savings plans, child development centers, life and disability insurance policies, and adoption assistance. Supplemental benefits include legal aid, home and auto insurance, and flexible spending accounts.

Park Place Entertainment is a gaming establishment that operates and manages 28 casino properties including Caesars, Paris, Bally's, Flamingo, Hilton and Grand Casinos. Hilton Hotels divided its gaming and lodging sectors to form two separate companies in 1998. Park Place has the most diverse gaming operation in the world and earns 4.7 billion in revenue annually.

Key Industry Events—Hotels, Restaurants, Casinos

There are hundreds of events, expos, conferences, and trade shows for the lodging, restaurant, and gaming industries. The larger expos and conventions host over 10,000 attendees, thousands of buyers, and hundreds of organizations. Many prominent speakers—including past U.S. presidents, star athletes, and well-known members of the hospitality industry—appear on the guest speaker rosters. There are many reasons why these conferences are worth attending. Insight into new best practices in the industry, the opportunity to try products and services not yet released to the public, and the chance to mingle with peers are just a few.

The National Restaurant Association's International Wine, Spirits and Beer Event and the Nightclub and Bar Convention and Trade Show are two of the industry's largest professional events focused exclusively on alcohol and beverage markets in the United States. The National Restaurant Association expo event features vintners, distillers, and brewers; food-alcohol pairing demonstrations; and educational demonstrations focused on trends in alcohol. The 2009 Nightclub and Bar Convention and Trade Show was held in Las Vegas and featured thousands of exhibitors showcasing food and beverage products and service providers. Show events often feature speakers and presentations designed to highlight business trends and practical advice for bar owners. Some specialty events even allow guests to mix their own new drink recipes.

The National Restaurant Association trade show is one of the largest in the industry. Its events offer restaurant owners and managers, culinary educators, and executive chefs at restaurants, hotels, and country clubs the opportunity to explore the latest food and beverage trends. The International Restaurant Show is another large exposition, taking place in Las Vegas.

There are other smaller, but still worthwhile, trade shows and conventions. The Craft Brewers Conference (called BrewExpo America) is the most important forum in North America for brewing education and idea-sharing to improve brewery quality and performance. The conference provides a social venue for craft brewers as well. Over 2,600 craft brews were featured at the 2008 Craft Brewer's Conference. This convention gives exhibitors and buyers the opportunity to develop business relationships while they learn more about brewing. Restaurant professionals are able to view the latest and the best that industry vendors have to offer.

HotelWorld is a large lodging-focused exposition whose goal is to host thousands of hotel professionals each year. This new expo, created in 2008, was designed specifically to offer products, marketing opportunities, and business innovations to professionals dedicated to the food and beverage markets within the lodging industry. Although it is a new expo, HotelWorld drew attendees from all over the United States, with a large representation from foreign countries. This expo is held in Las Vegas.

One of the oldest lodging trade shows and conventions is the International Hotel/Motel & Restaurant Show that has been held in New York City at the Jacob Javits Center for 94 years. This trade show sets aside an entire day for lodging exhibitions. The exhibits are typically in the categories of: décor (furniture, color coverings, artwork, draperies, signage, etc.), technology (software, security systems, HVAC, entertainment systems and waste and energy management), restaurant service equipment and furnishings, restaurant consulting, food and beverage products, and cleaning and maintenance supplies. This trade show has had in excess of 35,000 attendees, with over 1,000 exhibitors.

The largest gaming expo in the world is Global Gaming Expo, or G2E. It hosts between 700 and 1,000 exhibitors, showcasing hundreds of products over a three-day period in Las Vegas. In addition to several hundred conferences, gaming institutes offer education courses in leadership, casino design, and security systems and surveillance techniques. There are also specialty events focused on the food and beverage industry within the casino industry and entertainment other than gambling in the casino industry. The expo typically features celebrity appearances and keynote speakers who are leaders in the casino industry.

Legal Issues—Hotels, Casinos, Restaurants

All three sectors of the hospitality industry deal with overlapping legal issues: employee issues, customer complaints, and health violations. Still, each sector has its own legal problems to tackle. Below is a brief outline of legal issues faced by each sector.

The Employment of Minors

One of the biggest legal issues for restaurants and hotels is the hiring of minors, which means anyone under the age of 18. Federal law allows for minors at the age of 14 to be deemed employable during the school year—but only until 7:00 P.M. (They may work until 9 P.M. on school breaks and holidays.) Minors aged 16 and 17 are not subject to the number of hours they work, but they may not work in hazardous conditions or with any machinery. For restaurants, for example, this law would prevent a minor from operating a dough-mixer or meat-cutting machine. Likewise, for hotels, having minors operate tree-cutting or lawn-mowing machinery may be considered dangerous. Managers are responsible for the hiring and supervision of employees, and must check identification for the age of minors, be familiar with the jobs they can and cannot perform, and limit their working hours by law. Managers should also run periodic checkups to identify any problems with compliance with the above restrictions.

The American with Disabilities Act

The American with Disabilities Act (ADA) was passed in 1990. It is a disability discrimination law that prohibits employers, in most circumstances, from allowing an individual's handicap to negatively impact his or her career. An individual with a disability can get protection under the ADA if he or she can prove a physical or mental impairment that substantially limits one or more major life activities. Title III of the ADA, which requires the removal of barriers that prevent persons with disabilities from full and equal access to public accommodations, applies to hotels and restaurants. Customers with disabilities must have full access to restrooms, dining areas, guest rooms, doorways, parking lots, swimming pools, and laundry rooms. They must also be provided with accommodations for service animals and access to ice machines and listening devices for telephones, computers, and cash machines. Warning lights must be placed on irons and other potentially dangerous appliances for the hearing impaired, and braille on appliances and other items for the visually impaired. According to Title III, restaurant and hotel employees must be trained in policies for assisting persons with disabilities.

The law provides for injunctive relief to stop ADA violations. California, Colorado, and Florida allow plaintiffs to recover actual, punitive, and statutory damages. In California, the mandatory minimum statutory damages are $4,000 per violation. Unfortunately, lawyers have taken full advantage of the law and have been suing hospitality establishments since the 1990s. Even after they have passed inspection by their local government agencies, hotels and restaurants are being sued for minor infractions. With litigation on the rise, restaurants and hotels are faced with increasing legal fees in addition to having to make changes to their properties.

To further complicate matters, the Department of Justice proposed new ADA accessibility guidelines for buildings and facilities. The changes threaten to pose major cost on restaurants and hotels. There are so many gray areas within the law that the National Restaurant Association has actually submitted formal complaints about the proposed changes.

Many in the hospitality industry are now lobbying for the ADA Notification Act, which would allow small businesses 90 days to correct an ADA violation. While the hospitality industry has made great strides in adjusting to the ADA—and has come a long way in terms of increasing accessibility provisions—there appears to be a need for a better balance between the current litigious climate, businesses compliance, and customers' essentials.

Health Inspections

A major area of concern for restaurants is passing health inspections. All restaurants must pass a health inspection in order to have an operating license. A restaurant manager must know the health codes for his or her state and town. Health inspectors can conduct three types of inspections: (1) a routine inspection (which is literally a drop-in visit), (2) a complaint inspection (where a customer lodges a complaint against a restaurant or becomes sick from eating at the restaurant), and (3) a follow-up inspection after a restaurant has been issued a warning of a violation.

The spread of bacteria and viruses can be devastating for a food service business, and the leading cause of food poisoning is poor employee hygiene. Cleanliness is also of utmost importance to a restaurant's reputation and profitability. Kitchens, dining rooms, and restrooms must all be cleaned and sanitized regularly. All employees must keep their hands washed and clean at all times. Restaurants must have clear instructions for the storing of cooked food and other products that need refrigeration, as well as for the cleaning of equipment and utensils. Other practices that need to be closely monitored are the proper labeling of food storage containers, the calibration of meat thermometers, the division of space between areas where employees change and equipment is stored, the thorough cleaning of dishes, and the proper storage of meat, poultry, and seafood (all of which must be chilled to the right temperature).

It is essential for employees to be schooled in food safety practices, and they must demonstrate that they know how to handle food safely. Employees who are ill, but can report to work, must be removed from handling food or utensils. Instructions on how to wash produce and chill meats, fish, poultry, and leftover food must be adhered to. There are also guidelines on how to gauge the right temperature to properly defrost, thaw, cook, and reheat food, as well as how to properly dispose of food and other waste.

Hotel Safety Codes

Hotels have similar health and safety requirements. Regular inspection and testing of portable electrical appliances such as hairdryers, kettles, irons, and televisions is critical. These appliances are subject to much wear and tear and, as such, require routine assessments.

There must be an organized system in place for the staff of housekeepers to follow. A definite no-no is bugs—bedbugs, termites, and roaches (or any other type of insect, for that matter!) are not acceptable in any kind of hotel. Frequent spraying and sanitization of mattresses, curtains, and other interior decorations made from fabric will ensure that bugs are not a problem. Waste and trash should be disposed of on a regular basis.

Hotel rooms should be cleaned daily, glassware used in bathrooms washed or replaced daily, and towels replaced daily (although some hotels offer their guests the opportunity to reuse their towels in the interest of being more environmentally friendly). Towel service is a must after each change of guest in a room. Carpets and furniture need to be positioned so that guests do not trip and fall on them. Television brackets or shelves that hang overhead may pose safety hazards and should be given consideration. Windows should not open beyond a certain measure, as a safety precaution, and slip mats and rails in the bathtubs should be available to help prevent slipping and falling. (Ideally, floor surfaces should be made of non-slip material.)

The water temperature throughout the hotel water system should never reach scalding. *Legionella* is a type of bacteria commonly found in water systems, fountains, faucets, and HVAC systems. Regular testing of a hotel's water and regular sanitization of its fountains and HVAC systems is crucial.

Some other basic hygiene and safety concerns include patios, tennis courts, gyms, and swimming pools. Swimming pools must be properly maintained. Safe storage for chemicals is critical. Training of staff and adequate supervision of a pool by lifeguards is crucial for pool safety. Water disinfection is also important. The water's pH must be tested daily, and records of such tests must be kept. Adequate signage for unauthorized entry or use should be posted. Health and fitness centers should always have someone on duty to supervise guests and assist them with equipment. Equipment must be correctly installed, maintained, and inspected on a regular basis. Hotels that allow pets and smokers must take extra care to clean up stains or mend burns left behind after guest departures.

Other safety concerns of which hotel managers must be aware include exposed electrical cords, wet floors, and spills in public areas such as stairs and landings. Elevators and food lifts must be inspected and maintained regularly. Managers should immediately address broken windows and loose doors and windows. Fire codes must be adhered to according to state standards. The fire safety code depends on the size, age, and height of a hotel structure. Newer hotels and high-rise hotels are protected with fire sprinklers. Some hotel owners have corporate policies to retrofit older properties with fire sprinklers. Hotels must install well-maintained fire alarm systems that do not create false alarm problems. Standpipes and hoses must be installed at various points in the hotel. Fire extinguishers must be readily available to employees and guests, and fire exits must be easy to see and lighted at all times.

INTERVIEW

Opportunities in the Industry

Cara Lane,
Restaurant Manager, The Salvation Café, Newport, Rhode Island

How long have you worked in the restaurant business? What does your current job entail?
I've worked in restaurants for over 10 years. Currently, I manage a busy restaurant in Newport, Rhode Island, and oversee just about everything except for the cooking: from marketing and customer service to scheduling, supply ordering and maintenance issues. But a big part of my job is simply being a liaison between the owner, the kitchen staff, and the floor staff.

Would you say that there is a higher or lower percentage of workers with formal/academic restaurant training in your workplace? To what do you attribute your response?
Most of our front-of-house (servers, bartenders, bussers) are college-educated—and although it is not a job requirement, it helps. The kitchen managers (executive and sous chef) have formal culinary training while most of the others (line and prep cooks and dishwashers) may have a wealth of cooking experience but simply high-school educations. When a chef has formal culinary training, it usually guarantees that this a career for him or her and not just a stopover.

Are there any roles within the restaurant industry with more exciting trajectories than others in your opinion? Do any restaurant roles have fewer opportunities for those looking to climb the workplace ladder?
My job is unpredictable and that keeps it exciting. But I think the executive chef and the sous chef have amazing opportunities. They have the freedom to experiment with food in every way imaginable and are the true artists here. Most of us in the restaurant business share a love of food and have the most respect for our chefs. And when a food establishment gets written about, it is usually based on the menu and those who create it. A great chef will get noticed and can choose where he or she wants to go with it.

Those washing dishes may only move on to becoming a prep cook or, if they are dedicated and talented, may move on to line cooking.

Rarely would they move on to head chef positions, so their mobility is somewhat limited.

In what ways do you think the economic downturn of 2008-2009 affected the restaurant business as a whole?
I understand that the industry standard shows a 15 percent decline in net sales for 2008–2009. Fortunately, we have experienced the exact opposite: a 15 to 25 percent increase in sales over our previous year. We have had to respond to the downturn in creative ways: offering discounts on slower nights and not raising prices but, in many cases, actually lowering our prices. I think that any restaurant that wants to survive must respond to its customers' needs in this case, that means making it affordable to eat out and making the customer feel that the experience was worth return visits. Essentially, you need to offer better food at a better value. There is very little room for error at this point.

Are there other aspects about our world today (societal trends, for instance) that have played a role in shaping today's food service establishments?
With the widespread popularity of gourmet food shows on television this past decade, I think that many diners have begun to fancy themselves gourmands. They are knowledgeable about food ingredients and preparation, they are willing to try new ingredients, and they expect the best. In order to satisfy savvy, modern diners, a good chef must master simplified, classic cooking but should also remain adventurous. The front of the house needs to excite, as well. While most customers simply want a good meal, many appreciate a level of entertainment. They will linger longer—and, more importantly, they will return—if they enjoy the overall experience.

What tips might you offer a person contemplating a job in today's food service industry?
Anyone contemplating a job in a good restaurant should realize that, while unpredictable and therefore exciting, it can be a very stressful environment. We do joke that a busy night at a restaurant feels much like the pace of an ER so you need to come prepared: Hungry people can be grouchy, chefs will always be hot-tempered and servers and bartenders are depending on both to make their living. I think it is important to know yourself well and learn to know other people even better. This will help you respond rationally and respectfully to the constant demands of those around you.

The quality of fire protection varies by region. In some areas, building and fire officials keep their safety codes current and diligently enforced. But code advancement and enforcement are not uniform across the United States. Needless to say, if these codes are not kept up-to-date and enforced by competent personnel, the quality of fire safety can suffer greatly.

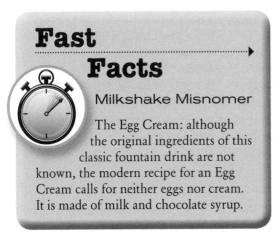

Fast Facts

Milkshake Misnomer

The Egg Cream: although the original ingredients of this classic fountain drink are not known, the modern recipe for an Egg Cream calls for neither eggs nor cream. It is made of milk and chocolate syrup.

Along with customer health and safety at their hotels, managers must also concern themselves with the health and safety of their employees. Safe and ergonomic equipment helps prevent injuries to workers. Because much of a hotel's workforce is often young, managers must target this population's education on safety in the workplace. About 45 percent of 16 and 17-year-olds are employed in the workforce at any given time, and an estimated 80 percent are employed at some point before they leave high school. Approximately 200,000 of these young workers are injured each year. Given these high numbers, the Occupation Safety and Health Administration implemented a Young Worker Initiative, the goal of which is to increase young workers' awareness of the importance of occupational safety and health.

Legal Issues for Casinos

Casinos have their own set of unique legal issues not faced by hotels or restaurants. Casinos, in particular, must work towards detecting funds procured illegally or from illegal activity. Casinos pay close attention to the behavior of gamers on the floors and watch for suspicious movement or activity. Money laundering is an illegal activity not uncommon in casinos. Gaming operations must assist law enforcement agencies in identifying and combating money laundering. Other issues of concern within casinos include excessive alcohol use while gambling and underage gambling.

Chapter 3

On the Job

The hospitality industry employs thousands of people in a huge variety of professions. The operations within the industry are like machines that run smoothly only through precise synchronization of their various parts. From the hotel manager to the bellhop, or from the restaurant manager to the dishwasher, each employee must perform his or her duties with stellar efficiency to maximize guest satisfaction. Only then can an establishment feel confident that its guests will return and that it will benefit from favorable reviews and word-of-mouth recommendations.

This chapter provides an up-close look at each of the roles that plays a part in an establishment's success. The first section in this chapter discusses managerial jobs at hotels and inns, followed by nonmanagerial jobs and then jobs in specialty hotels. Hotels are big operations, and these three categories are sufficiently different from each other to warrant separate sections. Since restaurants are smaller-scale operations, all restaurant positions are grouped together in one section, which follows the three sections about hotel jobs. Within each section, positions are discussed in alphabetical order.

Managerial Jobs at Hotels and Inns

The following managerial positions require sound leadership skills, including the ability to effectively delegate tasks to staff members.

Banquet Manager

A banquet manager is responsible for ensuring that food and liquor costs are in check and that a hotel is not overspending. He or she also prepares reports for budgeting purposes, completes daily staff attendance registers, and when necessary, trains staff.

It is the banquet manager's responsibility to make sure that when a booking is confirmed, all details are in place to ensure that the event will run smoothly. An inventory must be completed to guarantee that all items required are accounted for: the number of staff needed; the type of service required; the menu to be prepared; that everyone on the guest list has a seat; that drinks, aperitifs, and other specialty items are ordered; and that the live entertainment or audio equipment is checked and in order. The banquet manager must meet with the client to review the details of an event and gain the client's approval and confidence that things will run smoothly.

On the day of a booked event, the banquet manager must check to make sure that the staff is punctual, neatly attired, fully-briefed on the expectations for the day/evening, and ready to be of service to guests. There must be a quick review of all restrooms, powder rooms, and dining and lounge areas to confirm they have been neatly appointed—floral arrangements are in place, the bar service is fully stocked and ready to serve—and then he or she must handle any potential last minute snags. During the function, the banquet manager should circulate and check to see that guests are comfortable and happy. Once the event or function has ended, the banquet manager is responsible for the storage of extra equipment as well as ensuring that all furniture, food, and other items have been accounted for and properly put away. The banquet manager must also respond to guest inquiries, letters, and comments regarding the event.

The banquet manager shares the second-highest rung on the hierarchical ladder of the hotel with the front of house manager and night manager.

Front of House Manager

Front of house is a term used in the hospitality industry that pertains to areas of guest interaction. Examples of places *not* considered "front of house" are kitchens and housekeeping storage. The front of house (FOH) manager is responsible for the aesthetics, attractiveness, and cleanliness of any and all hotel areas that are visible to guests. The FOH manager has the responsibility to see that guests receive good customer service. He or she also oversees efficiency in the service of food and beverages and other items needed by guests. Room service orders must be filled in a prompt manner. Dining rooms and tables must be clean and well appointed. Guest rooms, restrooms, and other areas in use by guests must be clean and comfortable.

The FOH manager is responsible for booking live entertainment for guests. Table reservation and room reservations are the most important intake processes for hotels and restaurants. These systems must be running efficiently and customers must be satisfied with their tables or rooms. The FOH manager should be visible to customers and guests, making frequent rounds in the dining rooms, bars, and lounge areas of the restaurants or hotels. The FOH manager is also responsible for back of the house operations, ensuring that the kitchen, housekeeping, grounds-keeping, and laundry operations run both smoothly and efficiently.

How the wait staff looks falls is still another responsibility of the FOH manager. The uniformed staff must be neatly dressed and behave in a courteous and professional manner. The FOH manager must make sure that wait staff is properly trained. He or she must support staff, always listening to their grievances. If necessary, the FOH manager must take disciplinary action against staff to highlight the importance of professionalism on the job at all times. It is essential that the staff understand what is expected of them as a team and service community. The FOH manager typically holds regular staff meetings to disseminate important information and facilitate open communication. Additionally, the FOH manager will need to conduct performance appraisals and identify instances where the staff needs training and development—and then provide the necessary training. The hiring and recruitment of qualified staff is also the FOH manager's responsibility.

The FOH manager is responsible for the ordering and storing of goods. He or she must direct staff to conduct stock inventories on a regular basis. When reports, inventories, and liquor licenses need to be filed or obtained, the FOH manager is in charge of doing so. The FOH manager must keep an eye on the expense budget so that cost control is in effect.

Last but not least, staff must be trained on how to proceed in the event of a fire, theft, or burglary, and it is the FOH manager's duty to ensure that they have been. Finally, the FOH manager must alert the staff to any breaches in security and ensure that all security monitoring is effective.

Hotel Manager (General Manager)

A hotel manager is generally responsible for the day-to-day management of a hotel. He or she is accountable for organizing and directing all hotel services, including front-of-house services, food and beverage operations, and housekeeping. In many larger hotels, managers often specialize within a general management team, in areas such as guest services, accounting, or marketing. In addition to devising strategies to maximize profits, a manager must also pay attention to details, serving as an example for staff with regard to a standard of service consistent with the guests' needs.

Hotel managers work either on-site (as front of house, food and beverage, banquet, room service, or night managers) or off-site (as a general manager who oversees all operations). The general manager and operations manager—at smaller establishments these positions may be fulfilled by a single person—are at the top of the hotel management pyramid.

Night Manager

A night manager's shift typically begins around midnight or 1 A.M., and he or she is responsible for the comfort of guests throughout the nighttime hours. The night manager is responsible for checking in late-arriving guests and ensuring that luggage is deposited quickly in their rooms. These late guests must also be made aware of the food and other services available both at night and in the morning. The night manager must make sure there is prompt room service for tired guests—guests who arrive at a late hour often use room service.

By checking rosters, a night manager can ensure that duties are correctly parsed out and jobs are getting done. He or she must check that night cleaning staff is performing to the standards of the hotel. Locking up is an essential night manager job. He or she checks that keys are replaced and the kitchen has been cleaned and properly closed up. He or she checks that all fires have been extinguished and stoves turned off. Nighttime staff members are visited in order to ensure no one is sleeping on the job. The night manager must also lock up all cash and floats in the main office.

In the morning, the night manager checks that early deliveries have arrived, early breakfast orders are promptly filled, notice boards are updated for the coming day, and reports on any incidents that occurred during the night are properly filed.

Operations Manager

The operations manager oversees the sales, profitability, staffing, training, and development of the staff within a region or area. The operations manager is responsible for the growth and profitability of the hotels in his or her district or region. He or she may also be held responsible for the hotel's image. The rating of a hotel is often measured by customer satisfaction. This position typically requires close attention paid to customer ratings and customer satisfaction, which, in turn, drives profitability.

The operations manager must make sure that each district under his or her management is creating revenue. He or she must understand how to work with staff in a professional manner, encouraging that employees are as effective and productive in their jobs as they can be. An operations manager must be a dynamic leader. He or she must conduct frequent performance appraisals, be supportive and helpful to subordinates, listen to staff needs, and be able to communicate effectively. Being a coach is a necessary part of the operations management position. The personnel manager and the operations manager often collaborate in order to create meaningful career goals and duties for the management positions they oversee. They must monitor and measure employee competence as well as draw plans to ensure that subordinate managers are achieving their career goals.

The operations manager must also ensure that district managers are likewise drawing up action plans and career goals for their subordinates and making frequent staff performance appraisals. By paying close attention to employee turnover, the operations manager can work toward reducing the loss of strong workers. Staff must be fully schooled in company policies and procedures. The operations manager must review and analyze work efficiency as well as rectify problems with work performance, and is the ultimate authority on salary raises.

Profit margins are of utmost importance to an operations manager. He or she must make sure that debts are collected and purchases are being made at discount rates. The operation manager must decide on reasonable budgets by analyzing the state of the industry and gauging how his or her operation will perform based on market research. This requires that he or she keep in close contact with sales managers, working with them to create realistic sales quotas and proposals.

Customer relations is another area of responsibility for the operation manager. He or she must act quickly to correct problems experienced by customers. It is also worthwhile for the operations manager to attend company events, including social affairs and promotional/marketing events. He or she should be visible to clients.

Best Practice

The Benefit of a Second Language

Learning a foreign language increases a job seeker's marketability and expands opportunities to work in the international market.

Industry trends are an important factor in how well a hotel will run and the operations manager must be aware of any and all of the changes occurring in the industry. He or she must make wise decisions related to the implementation of new ideas based on trends that may benefit his or her company.

Just like the staff, sales, and district managers, the operations manager is required to attend meetings and training events while constantly searching for ways to improve his or her own professional skills in order to continue being an effective leader for his or her hotel.

Room Service Manager

The room service manager oversees and supervises the running of all room service areas within the confines of the hotel. The room service manager must be sure that all trays and trolleys are laid out in a pleasing manner. He or she must review the staff's appearance as well as ensure that food prep lines are ready to facilitate quick preparation. The room service manager makes certain that furniture is removed or replaced as needed, and any special cleaning arrangements are done through him or her.

That cash transactions occur correctly and all bills are signed is the room service manager's responsibility. He or she must also make sure inventory is done on a regular basis, the restocking of goods take place as needed, and maintenance is done on all equipment.

The room service manager typically works under the supervision of the banquet and general managers and is considered a stepping-stone position to one of those two more-senior positions.

Nonmanagerial Hotel Positions

In the world of hospitality, the entire staff must function together to ensure a high quality of service that will draw repeat customers. The following positions are essential to making sure everything runs smoothly during a guest's visit.

Bellhop

A bellhop escorts hotel guests to their rooms and carries their luggage. He or she also makes sure that rooms are in order and procures any extra items requested by guests. Bellhops also set up furniture and coffee service for functions. Finally, bellhops sometimes handle complaints, run errands for guests, and respond to service requests.

Bookkeeper

The bookkeeper's daily workload consists of compiling and completing all financial transactions for the day, as well as tracking and recording all weekly and monthly reports and returns. The bookkeeper reconciles and balances cash expenditures and income; reviews balance sheets, floats and dockets; and tallies daily expenses. The bookkeeper must keep the management alert to any record anomalies. He or she can also make payments from petty cash with the correct presentation of vouchers and invoices. The bookkeeper handles all stocktaking figures and assists in stocktaking at the prescribed times.

All safes and money drawers must be checked and securely locked. Documentation must be kept in places safe from fire and theft, and it is the bookkeeper's job to keep track of these documents. He or she also keeps abreast with training and development, attends management meetings, and is aware of the control systems in place to keep purchasing and revenues in order and within the agreed-upon budgets of the company.

Butler

Butler service is typically found in luxury hotels. Butlers give personalized service that often exceeds guest expectations. Butlers may need to book events or restaurant reservations. They may provide cocktail service if guests hold parties in their rooms. Some hotels have bath butlers; these people draw baths, sprinkle scents, and provide edibles while the guest soaks. Butlers may sometimes be asked to press clothes, shine shoes, or check for lint on suits and other items. At luxury hotels, butlers look and act much like personal valets.

Concierge

The concierge provides information and special services designed to enhance guests' visits. This position includes myriad responsibilities, from booking exclusive theatre tickets to giving directions to local events. Concierges communicate directly with guests, providing information on facilities and services, events and attractions, and transportation options.

Desk Clerk

The front desk clerk greets, registers, and assigns rooms to guests, issues room keys, makes and confirms reservations, and sorts incoming mail and messages. He or she is further responsible for transmitting and receiving phone messages, fielding inquiries pertaining to hotel services, and keeping track of room availability and guests' accounts. Desk clerks must be quick-thinking, energetic, and team-oriented. Hotel managers typically look for these characteristics when hiring desk clerks. Good spelling and computer literacy are also of paramount importance. Foreign language fluency is a definite plus because of the increasing international clientele at many establishments.

Diligent performance in the duties of desk clerk will often lead to a promotion to head receptionist and, eventually, a managerial position.

Head Porter and Doorman

The head porter and doorman positions overlap in many hotels. In a large hotel, the head porter supervises the doorman. The porter and the doorman are two of the first faces a guest sees upon his or her arrival at a hotel and, as such, must be pleasant people, always greeting hotel guests with cheer and enthusiasm. The head porter's responsibilities include meeting and greeting guests, opening doors, and arranging guest transportation. He or she may give directions to local attractions and points of interest, and he or she is the last person the guests sees when leaving the facility. Bidding fond farewells to guests is not to be taken lightly by someone in this position.

The head porter also stores bags, maintains bag tags, and notifies maintenance of any necessary repairs. The head porter may need to tactfully control a rowdy guest and have him or her escorted to his or her rooms, or ask unwanted intruders to leave the lobby area of the hotel. Occasionally, he or she may need to act as security detail for an important guest.

The head porter also coordinates department meetings and arranges the allocation of work stations to other porters and bell hops. In addition to opening and closing doors, he or she is in charge of keeping the lobby area clean. General traffic and parking on hotel property is also supervised by the head porter.

Head Receptionist

The head receptionist oversees all registrations and room allocations for guests. He or she is visible to the guests and is often responsible for the first impression made on a guest of a hotel. The head receptionist checks over the duty rosters and makes sure that all jobs are covered with sufficient staffing, makes the necessary arrangements to cover the responsibility of absent staff members, and handles complaints at the time of check in.

The head receptionist is neat in appearance and enthusiastic, and must ensure that the reception area staff appear likewise. He or she is responsible for guests having an easy, hassle-free check in and checkout, and will often work with the office and housekeeping to assist guests with their needs. He or she must be made aware of room changes and keep housekeeping and the telephone room apprised of any and all such modifications.

The guest register must be updated regularly throughout the day as guests arrive and leave the hotel. The head receptionist sends copies of the updated list throughout the day to various other departments. He or she handles maximum room occupancy policies of the hotel and attempts to adhere to the hotel's overbooking policies. Fully aware of all security measures used by the hotel, the head receptionist is able to effectively proceed with these policies in case of an emergency. He or she is also responsible for staff training and development, and participates in career appraisals of line staff in collaboration with management.

The head receptionist is the highest sub-managerial position at the hotel, and is highly desirable for anyone with managerial ambitions.

Housekeeping Supervisor

A housekeeping supervisor oversees the housekeeping staff, assigning their individual duties and responsibilities. He or she investigates and addresses complaints from staff members. The housekeeping supervisor may be involved in the hiring of housekeeping staff, and is often responsible for their training. In the case of a shortage of housekeepers, the supervisor may need to step in and assume the role of a maid. The housekeeping supervisor purchases housekeeping supplies and equipment and takes inventory of needed supplies. The housekeeping supervisor also informs the desk as to which rooms are ready for occupancy after cleaning. Lastly, he or she keeps records and prepares written reports for management.

Laundry Room Attendant

The laundry room is divided into two areas of operation: (1) sorting and washing, and (2) drying and folding. A laundry room attendant separates dirty linens and loads the washers. He or she may then pass the wet laundry onto another attendant in charge of drying and folding. Laundry room attendants may also take in wash for individual guests, completing the entire job from washing to folding.

Linen Room Attendant

The linen room attendant distributes bed and table linens and uniforms. This attendant stores and keeps inventory of all linens within a hotel. The linen room attendant may receive dirty laundry from guest rooms, uniforms from employees, and linens from the hotel restaurant, then sending them to the laundry room. He or she is responsible for filling the housekeeping trolleys and cart and also requests the replacement of worn linens and other items that cannot be mended by the hotel seamstress or sewer.

Maid

A maid (or housekeeper) in a hotel must clean the guestrooms, hallways, lounges, lobbies, locker rooms, and all other areas in his or her charge. He or she must vacuum, change linens and towels, clean bathrooms, replace drinking glasses, and replenish stationery and complimentary grooming and food items provided for the guests. Maids handle trash disposal in all rooms, dust and clean all areas, replace light bulbs, and polish furniture as necessary. Maids may take guest laundry to dry cleaners as well as take guests' clothes to be pressed or repaired. They occasionally bring televisions, extra beds, baby cribs, and ironing boards to guests.

Maids may also be responsible for other hotel cleaning responsibilities, such as cleaning silverware, hanging curtains, changing mattresses, arranging furniture, disinfecting equipment, and using steam sterilizers. Sometimes maids are responsible for cleaning linens, ironing, sorting and loading washing machines, and folding dried clothing.

While the maid's position is typically entry-level, superlative attention to one's duties can lead to promotion to housekeeping supervisor.

Night Auditor

A night auditor keeps records and balances entries or keeps track of any financial transactions that occur during a hotel's day shifts. He or she may also do bookkeeping for the accounting office and sub-

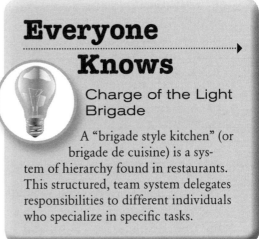

Everyone Knows

Charge of the Light Brigade

A "brigade style kitchen" (or brigade de cuisine) is a system of hierarchy found in restaurants. This structured, team system delegates responsibilities to different individuals who specialize in specific tasks.

stitute as the hotel desk clerk in smaller hotels. This position provides valuable experience for anyone seeking eventual entry to the managerial ranks—particularly for those whose sights are set on the role of operations manager.

Seamstress/Sewer

A hotel sewer or seamstress is responsible for repairing bed linens and guest clothing on request. This position requires someone highly skilled at using a sewing machine and at mending clothing by hand. He or she must be able to work quickly, and often under pressure, when guests need rapid repairs on clothing.

Switchboard Operators

Switchboard operators typically handle incoming, out-going, inter-office, and inter-room calls. They may also take messages for guests or announce visitors in the hotel. Many of the jobs performed by switchboard operators have become automated through the use of automated assisted directories and voicemail. Still, customers do sometimes prefer the assistance of switchboard operators.

Sometimes hotel guests do not know what departments or people they need to speak to. Frequently, guests require help with placing calls outside of the hotel because they do not know the proper codes to dial required by the region of the country where they are staying.

Switchboard operators are still also essential in the transmitting of communications for guests. Because nothing is simpler than dialing "0" for help, guests are reluctant to give up this convenience. Many hotels have switchboard operators available 24 hours a day, seven days a week. Sometimes, operators will work only during peak hours or busy periods to handle the high volume of calls. Peak times for switchboard operators include holidays and occasions when special events are occurring in the vicinity of the hotel.

Turn Down Attendant

The turn down attendant is personally responsible for checking that rooms are cleaned and well-stocked. He or she also "turns down" the beds at night for guests and stores large bedspreads and other items during the day. The turn down attendant sometimes fills ice buckets and brings specialized bottled items and snacks for gifts as requested by guests. This type of position is usually found within large or luxury hotels.

Jobs at Specialty Hotels

As previously mentioned, there are certain standard jobs found in every hotel. But in niche market hotels, there are, accordingly, more unique employee opportunities.

Hair Technician

A hair technician at a hotel spa needs to have a license and accreditation. A hair technician will be versed in cutting and styling hair as well as coloring and permanent techniques.

Massage Therapist

Many hotels have added spas to their list of guest services. Jobs available in spas require that job seekers to have specific set of skills. Massage therapy is one of the most popular spa services. Massage therapy is defined as "the manipulation of muscles to improve circulation, eliminate pain, and treat sore muscles and tension." A massage therapist must be accredited and licensed to work at a spa. Massage therapists can be both male and female, with guests sometimes requesting one over the other. Massage therapists must be familiar with all forms of massage therapies: sports, hot stone, deep tissue, pre-natal, foot, and Swedish.

Nail Technician

A nail technician must have a license and accreditation to work at a hotel spa. He or she performs manicures and pedicures.

Skin Care Esthetician

A skin care technician offers facial treatments, waxing, and other types of skin care treatments to guests. He or she must be familiar with all kinds of products and procedures on the cosmetics market. A motivated individual could seek to gain familiarity with the skills required to work as both a skin care esthetician and a nail technician.

Spa Attendant

A spa attendant is responsible for cleaning the massage rooms, waxing rooms, hair salon, and manicure/pedicure areas. He or she restocks towels, linens, and changes the linens after guests receive treatment. The spa attendant refills refreshments for guests and keeps the inventory stocked both for amenities and refreshments. The spa attendant fulfills guests' requests for service in a friendly and courteous manner. Services for guests while at the spa may include bringing refreshments, magazines, robes, or guests' personal effects to them. The spa attendant also runs errands for the other spa workers.

Spa Front Desk Attendant

This job requires an individual who is friendly and can handle guests' requests and complaints with poise. The front desk attendant checks guests into the spa, books appointments, and relays messages for guests and workers in the spa. The front desk attendant is also responsible for handling emergencies that arise for guests. Finally, this attendant performs clerical tasks, puts keys away, and locks up the spa area at night. Front desk attendants in the spa often aspire to either front desk positions in the hotel itself, managerial positions within the spa, or both.

Spa Supervisor

A supervisor oversees the running of the spa. He or she makes sure that appointments are booked, monies are correctly collected and recorded, and customers are receiving adequate care and attention as per the hotel's standards. This individual must be familiar with all of jobs within the spa and know which skills are needed to perform each one. The spa supervisor also interviews potential job candidates for positions at the spa, conducts performance reviews, and holds training sessions for employees. A spa supervisor may have supervision credentials, have risen through the ranks, or have prior experience. The advantage of having spa supervisor credentials makes someone interested in this position much more marketable to hotels and resorts that offer better wages and benefits.

Restaurant Jobs

Though the service and presentation of food often appears effortless to those of us on the consuming end, the reality is that the inner-workings of a restaurant demand the efficiency and precision of many different people.

Barback

A barback is a bartender's assistant. Barbacks work in nightclubs, bars, restaurants, and catering halls. Barbacks stock bars with liquor, ice, glassware, beer, garnishes, and so on—and usually receive a portion of the bartender's tips (often 10 percent to 20 percent). Bar-backs apprentice under the tutelage of bartenders and eventually work their way into the position. Typically, their primary responsibility is to simplify a bartender's job. Dishwashing and bussing tables are also common barback tasks. A great deal of experience in bussing is often required before one earns the position of barback, depending on the type and pace of the bar in question.

In the United States, the legal drinking age is 21. However, the legal age for working as a bartender or barback varies from 18 to 21. In high-volume bars and nightclubs, the barback is indispensable—he or she is not only an assistant, but an integral and invaluable member of the team. Most nightclub barbacks not only stock and continually re-stock glassware, but they also set up and tear down the face of the bar. The barback often begins working hours before the bartender arrives, and is still working for some time after the bartender is done. The barback may also be involved with a bar's inventory control, which typically means reporting opening and closing levels by weighing liquor bottles and making bottle counts.

It goes without saying that working as a barback provides invaluable hands-on experience for anyone with aspirations of working as a bartender.

Bartender

Bartenders prepare alcoholic drinks for patrons of restaurants, bars, cocktail lounges, and other establishments where drinks are served. Sometimes alcoholic drinks consist of multiple ingredients, and different drinks can be made in different ways. The bartender's main job is to know the standard drink recipes and to be able to mix them quickly and accurately. Occasionally, customers have their own preferences or recipes for a bartender to follow. Bartenders also check the identification cards of customers seated at bars to ensure that they are of minimum drinking age.

In restaurants, bartenders fill drink orders placed by diners (but the drinks are usually served by waiters). Additional bartending duties include arranging bottles and barware, washing glasses, and cleaning the bars. Bartenders also remove empty bottles and trash and replace empty beer kegs. In large bars and restaurants, bartenders may be assisted by barbacks.

Bartenders stock bars with liquor bottles, drink ingredients, garnishes, and other supplies. They keep track of wines, beers, and liquors. Some bartenders do the actual ordering of bar supplies. Others report what is needed to an owner or purchasing agent. In very large restaurants and bars, ordering supplies is the responsibility of a wine steward or a beverage manager.

In addition to bars and cocktail lounges, bartenders work in hotels and private clubs, aboard ships, and on trains. Many bartenders work in restaurants that have liquor licenses. About one-fifth of all bartenders own their own bars.

Busser (Busboy)

This is an ideal job for a high school student or someone interested in learning the restaurant business from the ground up. The busser's main job is to clear and set the dining room tables. However, he or she can be conscripted by the cooks to fetch ingredients that are running low, or by wait staff to assist with preparation of desserts or salads. The bartender may ask a busser to restock his coolers if he does not have his own barback. Working in a bussing position is an excellent way to gain exposure to all parts of the restaurant business—and a good transition to either a front of the house or back of the house position.

Dishwasher

Sparkling glasses and clean silverware make a good impression on restaurant customers. A clean table setting suggests a restaurant will offer good service and wholesome food. The person responsible for providing clean tableware is the dishwasher. After customers have completed their meal, a busser takes the dirty dishes to the dishwasher. Dishwashers scrape, sort, and stack dishes before loading them into dishwashing machines. Dishwashers fill the machines with soap and then turn them on. When the dishes are clean, dishwashers unload them and put them in their proper places so that other kitchen workers and waiters and waitresses can find them.

In very large establishments, dishwashers may perform only one or two jobs. For example, one dishwasher may scrape plates, while another dishwasher may be in charge of washing large pots and pans. Dishwashers are often responsible for additional cleaning jobs. Sometimes they clean floors, cabinets, sinks, and countertops. Dishwashers work in every establishment that serves food, including restaurants, buffets, hotels, coffee shops, hospitals, and schools.

Executive Chef (Head Chef)

The executive chef is the *capo de tutti capo*—or "boss of all bosses." He or she manages all other chefs and cooks, plans the menu, and ensures that food leaving the kitchen is consistently delicious and beautifully presented. He or she makes sure employees follow safety procedures and sanitation ordinances, and is typically responsible for recruiting, hiring, training, and firing kitchen staff. Executive chefs are on their feet for hours at a time, work long days and weekends, and seldom get a holiday off. They arrive at work early to receive deliveries and stay late to ensure that the kitchen is clean and fully prepared for the next day. They also manage a large group of cooks and chefs during many busy, stressful service periods each day. The responsibilities are huge—but so is the autonomy. As an executive chef, you operate your kitchen as you see fit (with little or no supervision) to produce the highest-quality cuisine.

In addition to planning menus and cooking, an executive chef also must hone his or her public-relations skills. Remaining vigilant with regard to customers' needs and the latest industry trends can keep a restaurant packed with customers.

Still, even executive chefs must sometimes participate in tedious activities, from handling special menu requests to calling out orders. Reviewing the daily roster of tasks is important, because the head chef needs to be sure those tasks have been evenly distributed. Executive chefs should be prepared to market a restaurant by representing it in the public forum. Establishing and maintaining good relationships with suppliers assures that the restaurant will benefit from better discounts and contract terms.

The titles *executive chef* and *head chef* are not always synonymous. If the executive chef is in charge of multiple locations, he or she may do less cooking and serve in more of an administrative capacity. In such a case, a head chef will be designated at each location and the executive chef will devote his or her time primarily to menu planning and supervisory duties.

Fish Chef (Poissonier)

The poissonnier is responsible for most of the cooking, garnishing, and sauce preparation for the fish courses on a menu, including freshwater and saltwater fish, and shellfish such as crabs, crayfish, shrimps, scallops, lobsters, and mussels. However, there are exceptions: deep-fried fish are normally attended to by an assistant cook, fish grilling is often done by the grill cook, and raw oysters are ordinarily served directly from the fishmonger (only when cooked are they plated directly by the poissonnier).

The poissonnier works on a stove section in the main kitchen. This means that cleaning, scaling, gutting, skinning, filleting, portioning, and bread crumbing are not done by the poissonnier but by someone else beforehand (typically a prep cook). It is sometimes arranged, however, for an assistant poissonnier to assist in these functions.

Host

Restaurant hosts and hostesses are the personal representatives of the restaurants where they work. They are in charge of taking reservations and greeting guests when they arrive at the restaurant. They also seat the guests and make sure that they are comfortable.

Hosts and hostesses try to give guests a good impression of the restaurant by greeting them in a warm, cordial manner. If guests must wait to be seated, hosts and hostesses make them comfortable while they wait. Guests should be told how long they will have to wait and are seated at the bar or in a waiting area. Hosts and hostesses locate a table that is the right size for the guests, take the guests to the table, and distribute menus. They may also assist guests in seating small children, taking drink orders, or filling water glasses.

While greeting incoming guests, hosts and hostesses must also attend to guests who are leaving. Some hosts and hostesses take money and make change. At the end of a work shift, hosts and hostesses record the transactions during the course of that shift and total the guest checks to determine how much money has been received. These records are used to balance the accounts at the end of the day.

A host's daily interaction with customers and familiarity with all aspects of restaurant operations makes him or her an ideal candidate for eventual promotion to front of house manager.

Line Cooks (Chefs de Partie)

A line cook works under the sous chef and specializes in a culinary component such as sauces, fish, roasting, grilling, frying, butchering, vegetables and side dishes, salads, and appetizers. Line cooks are on their feet at all times and work long hours, often including weekends and holidays. Service periods, when large numbers of diners are ordering food, are especially hectic. However, one of the best aspects of working as a line cook is gaining expertise in an area of specialty. A good restaurant kitchen is like an efficient machine with no superfluous parts. Effective, efficient, knowledgeable line cooks are critical to the kitchen's operation. The primary chefs de partie include sauté chef, fish chef, roast chef, soup chef, vegetable chef, and pastry chef.

Pastry Chef (Pâtissier)

Pastry chefs specialize in baking and are considered a breed apart in most restaurants. In some larger restaurants, the pastry chef may supervise a separate team of bakers and may even manage a separate pastry kitchen. A pastry chef oversees the preparation of all fresh baked goods. Baking is different from other forms of cooking because a recipe must follow a sensitive and fixed chemical equation. Many variables, including the humidity and temperature of the ingredients and the oven, can easily affect a recipe's outcome.

This is the perfect job for those who like to awaken early and complete most of their work before lunchtime. It is also a job that comes with many perks. For instance, a patissier not only gets to experience the satisfaction that comes from turning a pile of raw ingredients into a beautiful array of warm, delectable treats before breakfast time—but also has the security of knowing there are plenty of exciting job opportunities available to him or her.

Being a pastry chef can be taxing, both mentally and physically. As such, the job requirements include a decent level of physical fitness, the ability to pay close attention to detail, and pride in one's work. Pastry chefs are employed in many different settings. Although the most obvious place for a pastry chef to look for a job would be a bakery, many hotels, restaurants, bistros, and casinos also employ pastry chefs.

Formal training, along with highly developed culinary abilities and, of course, a passion for cooking, are requirements for a successful career as a pâtissier. A pastry chef must also be creative in order to successfully create new types of pastries. A pastry chef's role is not always limited to creating pastries. Some pastry chefs are charged with managing junior kitchen staff members. Others are

responsible for ensuring that the kitchen remains clean and orga-
nized.Many pastry chefs perform additional administrative duties,
such as assisting with budget preparation and ordering supplies for
pastry making.

Prep Cook

The prep cook is an entry-level kitchen position ideally suited for an
aspiring chef. An aspiring chef will gain invaluable experience as a
prep cook that will, in time, prepare him or her to advance to the
next rung on a kitchen's ladder.

Although a prep cook receives an enormity of on-the-job training, it is often useful to have some sort of basic training courses in
the culinary arts. Prep cooks usually work under the command of a
senior member of the kitchen staff. In light of this fact, it is important for a prep cook to be able to accept constructive criticism. A
kitchen can be a high-pressure work environment, and a prep cook
will need to have thick skin to deal with the inevitable customer
complaints—as well as those from more senior chefs. A prep cook
must also accept that he or she will inevitably make many mistakes
in this entry-level position. He or she must be able to view those
mistakes as valuable learning experiences.

Despite being at the bottom of a kitchen's ladder, the prep cook
is an integral member of the staff. Although a prep cook has less
responsibility than other kitchen staff members, the work he or she
performs is nevertheless crucial to the success of the kitchen. For
this reason, the successful prep cook will learn how to work well in
a team environment, will take responsibility for his or her mistakes,
and will always pay attention to details.

A prep cook's role is to assist in the preparation of meals by chopping vegetables, making salads, and helping to put together entrees.
Although this role generally does not include any cooking duties, it
provides the ideal opportunity to develop many other types of skills
essential to becoming a chef. These skills include proficiency with a
wide range of kitchen tools and utensils, including chopping knives
and vegetable grinders.

In addition to his or her food preparation tasks, a prep cook may
also be responsible for a large number of smaller tasks. Such tasks
sometimes include ensuring proper storage of leftover food, emp-
tying trash, washing dishes, and testing the temperature of food
at specified intervals. On occasion, certain restaurants and other

establishments also require their prep cooks to set or clear tables and deliver dishes to patrons.

Restaurant Manager

All restaurant activities are the manager's responsibility. In some small restaurants, the managers are also the owners, handling the business end of the operation. They supervise food and beverage purchases, advertising, and hiring of staff. They may also greet guests and seat them, serve as cashier, and even cook. This is most often the case at small, family-run restaurants.

In larger restaurants, a managers' work is primarily administrative. While the executive chef is responsible for food preparation, the restaurant manager coordinates the work of the rest of the staff. In certain restaurants, particularly those in hotels, managers may deal mainly with department heads. Despite this administrative aspect of the job, restaurant managers still must have a thorough knowledge of food service. They must also understand accounting, budgeting, and banking. Managers may even be responsible for resolving engineering problems. Equipment used for cooking, lighting, and ventilation is expensive, and so they must know about the cost, installation, and maintenance of such equipment.

Though the responsibilities of restaurant managers vary, most include the organization of stock, the ordering of food supplies and equipment, the inspection of health and safety precautions, and the solving of employee or customer problems. Restaurant managers typically interview, hire, and supervise the training of·new staff members.

One of a restaurant manager's most important responsibilities is in the area of customer service. It is mandatory that guests receive prompt service in a professional, friendly manner. A restaurant manager needs the expertise and patience to deal with customers, no matter how rude or unreasonable that customer may be. When a patron has a legitimate complaint, the restaurant manager works to correct the problem so that the customer leaves happy and is likely to come back in the future.

Common responsibilities of a restaurant manager include: (1) overseeing the day-to-day operation of the restaurant including cleaning, floor plan lay-out, table settings, and theme of the restaurant; (2) hiring, training, supervising, promoting, and firing staff; (3) working with the chef or cook to determine menu plans on a daily basis and for special events, groups, and parties; (4) purchasing all items including food, beverages, equipment, and supplies; (5) managing all accounts payable and receivable, handling payroll, and hiring accountants or bookkeepers as necessary; (6) meeting, greeting, and getting feedback from customers; and (7) advertising and marketing the restaurant within the community.

Roast Chef (Rotissueur)

The work of the rotisseur has evolved over time more, perhaps, than that of any other restaurant worker. Roasting with a spit over an open fire has largely been replaced by oven roasting. Spit roasting has recently made a comeback with special electrical heating equipment, but its use is normally limited to certain appropriate foodstuffs, such as chicken.

While roasting equipment may have changed, the duties of the roast cook have largely remained the same. Foods to be roasted still cover a wide range of poultry, game, and meat. In large establishments, the joints, poultry, and game to be cooked are given basic preparatory treatment by a prep cook, rather than by the rotisseur. Meanwhile, the rotisseur is also responsible for savory items such as Welsh rarebit, hot sandwiches of the club sandwich type, and all stock for the gravies that accompany the roasts.

Dishes prepared by the roast cook are not as complex as many completed by the saucier or poissonnier, yet he or she should be skilled in many areas, including how to gauge the correct cooking temperatures of roasted items of varying sizes and kinds.

This section of the kitchen tends to be most physically taxing. Heavily-loaded roasting trays can only be handled comfortably and safely by a person of physical strength. In addition to the physical demand, this section is located in the main stove area, where many items of heating equipment are grouped together—making it one of the hottest areas in the kitchen.

Larger establishments may have additional specialists. For example, a chef trancheur (carver) may work under the direction of the rotisseur. The trancheur is normally skilled only in carving—not in cooking—and may operate at the hot service counter behind the scenes, at a buffet table in the dining room, or by patrolling the restaurant with a heated cart. In some establishments, the work of the grill cook is undertaken by a subordinate of the chef rotisseur. The specific skill required of a grill cook is to be able to prepare foods to order using traditional charcoal grills or more modern grills using electricity or gas.

Sauté Chef (Saucier)

The saucier's duties are very complex. He or she cooks, garnishes, and plates all meat, poultry, and game dishes—with the exception of those that are simply grilled or roasted (which are cooked by the rotisseur). The saucier is typically responsible for at least one of the "plats du jour," or specialties of the day. The work of the saucier, therefore, involves much more than the preparation of sauces, important as that may be. (In fact, the saucier does not prepare *every* sauce. The chef poissonnier—the fish chef—prepares the sauces and garnishes for all seafood menu items.)

The saucier is not only the preparer of the sauce section's foods, but rather the assembler of food that has been prepared and sometimes cooked by others. For example, when entrees require Italian pastas or vegetables as garnishes on the same dish, these will be sent to the saucier by the *entremetteur*, or server. The work of all parties in the kitchen is similarly interrelated, but the saucier performs the greatest percentage of this type of assembly work. Given the enormous range of possible entrees, the saucier's work covers a wide and diverse arena. As such, this role requires a substantial degree of training, experience, skill, and artistry. Many sauciers know enough to be able to forego the recipes and operate by memory alone—at least for their more commonly-prepared dishes. The saucier is subordinate only to the chef and the sous chef.

Sommelier

Typically found in high-end, sophisticated restaurants, the sommelier ensures that dining patrons are able to find wines within their budgets that also fit their tastes and complement their foods. A sommelier must possess a thorough understanding of how food and wine pairings affect the palate. He or she is responsible for buying and properly storing wine, working with diners to suggest wines that complement their food and are in accordance with their taste and budget, and serving each wine properly. Sommeliers are also expected to be knowledgeable about beer, distilled liquors, mineral water, and even which type of cigar or tobacco will complement a meal or a wine. Many sommeliers host wine tastings to educate wine lovers and attract them to a restaurant.

Sous Chef

The sous chef is located just below the executive chef in a kitchen's chain of command. As such, the sous chef plays a vital role in the successful operation of any commercial kitchen. The second-in-command, a sous chef has great responsibility. Therefore, he or she can typically position him- or herself to become the executive of a kitchen in time.

The sous chef is supervised only by the executive chef, and may be asked to perform any of the executive chef's tasks, including managing other chefs and cooks, planning menus, ordering supplies, maintaining sanitation and cleanliness, and overseeing the consistent quality of the food service. Because sous chefs are involved in every aspect of the kitchen's operation, they work long hours and get few days off. There are times when a sous chef is the first to arrive in the morning and the last to leave at night. But they also are typically given a free hand to manage their shift or station with minimal supervision and great latitude in decision-making.

The sous chef is responsible for planning and directing food preparation in a kitchen. This involves, to a large degree, supervising other kitchen staff, as well as remaining vigilant of problems that arise in the kitchen and seizing control of a situation at a moment's notice. The sous chef may also need to discipline underperforming staff members, as well as provide incentives for staff members to exceed the expectations of their particular roles.

Finally, the sous chef may also be responsible for staff scheduling and, depending on the establishment, may even have a hand in apprenticeship development planning. A major percentage of a sous chef's tasks, therefore, are administrative—often consuming up to a quarter of his or her work hours.

Soup Chef (Potager)

The potager is responsible for preparing all soups and their accompanying garnishes. Because the potager prepares the earliest course of lunch and dinner, this position's hours often begin (and end) a little earlier than those of the other cooks.

The work of the potager is key to a successful meal since the soup course creates the initial gastronomic impression of the meal as a whole. Potagers must be able to produce a wide array of soups including consommes (clear soups), cream soups, purees, broths, bisques (shellfish soups), and many specialty and national soups. Consommés alone can be composed of dozens of different flavorings and garnished in hundreds of ways. The ingredients used by the chef potager may be supplied by other parties—for example, stock for fish soups can come from the chef poissonnier—but a substantial amount of garnish preparation for the soup corner itself still remains his responsibility, requiring skillful use of the knife and other culinary tools.

Of particular importance is the preparation of a wide variety of vegetable adornments. As with all chefs, a cultivated palate is an important attribute of a potager, because the adjustment of seasonings and the completion of a soup requires personal judgment as well as technical skill.

Vegetable Chef (Entremetier)

The entremetier is concerned mainly with cooking vegetables—but also with preparing eggs, pasta, rice, and other starches. When these are served as separate courses, they are cooked and assembled in the entremetier's section. Other responsibilities may include passing vegetable garnishes to another partie for completion of a dish and sending items (such as cooked spaghetti and rice) to another chef as garnish for other dishes. The chef entremeteur also makes pancakes, often with batter supplied by the patissier.

Important as these items may be, they are not more significant than the vegetables prepared and cooked as accompaniments to the main meat, poultry, and game dishes. The proper cooking, flavoring, garnishing, and service of vegetables is of tremendous concern to an establishment's culinary reputation. Yet because of the nature of what is being cooked by the entremetier, the volume of food handled in this section is typically greater than that handled by any other. Cooking vegetables well in large quantities demands not only great experience and skill, but also a familiarity with a vast array of methods.

To facilitate vegetable preparation, the portion required for the side dishes is often separated from the a la carte vegetables. The peeling, cleaning, trimming, and other basic treatments of vegetables can be boring and time-consuming, but modern processing methods are reducing much of this workload in the kitchen.

Waiter

Waiters are the men and women who interact with customers, take orders, and serve food in restaurants. They are typically assigned a certain number of tables (a station) by the restaurant manager or the headwaiter. A waiter provides a copy of the restaurant's menu to each customer, often describing the preparation for the different meals on the menu. Waiters take down customers' orders so that chefs can prepare each dish consistently with guests' desires.

When the food is ready, waiters escort it from the kitchen to the tables (except in establishments that have food runners). A good waiter remembers what each person has ordered and places the correct dish in front of the person who ordered it. This level of service assures good tips and brings customers back to a restaurant.

Waiters should pay constant attention to their guests. Their tasks include refilling coffee cups and water glasses when they are empty and asking if guests would like to place additional orders. They also meticulously note the food and drink prices on their guests' checks. When patrons are ready to leave, waiters bring their checks to the table. In some restaurants, waiters handle guests' payments for meals. In other, less formal establishments, guests take their checks directly to a cashier.

There are many different kinds of restaurants, and a waiter's work varies accordingly. In fine dining restaurants, waiters are usually supervised by a headwaiter and must serve food in a formal way. Many high-end restaurants offer a specific style of cuisine, such as French, Greek, Italian, Japanese, or some other specialized cuisine. Waiters in these restaurants can often speak the corresponding language if asked to when describing each individual dish.

A completely different working atmosphere exists in other types of restaurants. Some waiters work in bars and nightclubs where alcoholic beverages are served. In smaller restaurants, waiters are expected to perform many additional duties. They may clean tables, clear dishes, and even set the tables with clean tablecloths, napkins, and silverware. Sometimes their prep work (or "side" work) includes filling the salt, pepper, and sugar containers. They may also stock glasses and silverware so they can be easily retrieved during a rush period. In larger restaurants, bussers typically perform these tasks.

Casino Jobs

A casino is an incredibly complex environment demanding the contributions of many workers in many different capacities in order to
function smoothly.

Gaming Cage Worker

Gaming cage workers, also known as "cage cashiers," work in casinos
and other gaming establishments. The "cage" where they work serves
as the central depository for the money, chips, and other paperwork
intrinsic to casino play. Cage workers are responsible for a vast array
of financial transactions, and they coordinate any necessary paperwork. They execute credit checks and verify credit references for
players seeking a house credit account. Cage workers also provide
gambling chips, tokens, or tickets to patrons or, when necessary, to
other casino workers for the purpose of resale to patrons. And, of
course, they exchange chips and tokens for cash. They may be called
upon to operate cash registers and computers to perform calcula-
tions and record transactions. At their shift's end, cage cashiers must
be sure that the books are balanced.

Because the industry is subject to such intense governmental
scrutiny, cage workers must abide by a plethora rules and regulations related to their handling of money. Large cash transactions, for
example, need to be reported to the Internal Revenue Service. When
determining whether to extend credit or cash a check, cage workers
must strictly adhere to a series of highly-detailed procedures.

Casino Cage Supervisor

The cage supervisor position is one of great responsibility, as it
requires close monitoring of all of the house's financial transactions and ensuring compliance with state and federal laws and
regulations.

The cage supervisor is responsible for the casino's bankroll as well
as the enforcement of the gaming rules and regulations within the
casino cage. He or she oversees all of the daily cash and credit receipts,
and all other disbursements by or within the casino cage. The cage
supervisor is further responsible for verification of all cash turned in
by each department, and maintains the returned check and marker
hold check files. The supervisor also supervises the casino cashiering

operation in strict compliance with individual internal controls and company procedures, and enforces the policies set forth by the federal cash reporting requirements.

Overseeing staff is another key element of the cage supervisor's job responsibilities. He or she hires the new employees and schedules, trains, and supervises all casino cage personnel. After reviewing staffing levels and monitoring customer flow, he or she then assigns work areas to the cage staff. The supervisor also oversees all checkout transactions and reviews cashiers' close-out procedures to ensure drawer balances and notes all discrepancies.

Gaming Dealer

Casino dealers may work in commercial casinos, pari-mutuel racetracks (also known as racinos), on riverboats, or in hotels. Each establishment sets its own requirements outlining necessary education, experience, and training, but all dealers must also obtain a license from a regulatory agency such as the State Casino Control Board or Gaming Commission.

Obtaining a gaming license is a multi-step process. A dealer must first offer proof of residency in his or her state. Applicants must then produce photo identification, pay a licensing fee and submit to a background investigation and drug test. Most establishments require a high school diploma or GED for most entry-level dealer positions. Some of the larger casinos operate their own casino schools, but nearly all offer in-house training in some form in addition to the required certification.

Some gaming dealers choose not to limit themselves to one state or even one country, choosing instead to pursue employment on luxury cruise liners that offer on-board casinos to customers as they travel the world. Dealers employed by cruise lines typically live and work on board the vessel.

The gaming dealer's job description typically includes most (if not all) of the following: exchanging money for playing chips; paying winners or collecting money from losers as per the rules and procedures of the specific game to which they are assigned; dealing cards to house hands and comparing them with players' hands to determine winners (usually in black jack); conducting gambling games including craps, roulette, cards, keno, or other games of chance according to the applicable rules and regulations; checking to make sure that players have placed bets before the start of play; standing behind the gaming table and dealing the required number of cards to the players; inspecting cards and gaming equipment to ensure that they are in proper working condition; starting and controlling games and equipment and announcing winning numbers or colors; opening and closing cash floats and game tables; computing players' wins or loss totals, and/or scanning winning tickets to calculate the amount for payout; applying rule variations to card games (i.e., poker) for which players bet according to the value of their individual hands; receiving, verifying, and recording wagers; fielding questions about game rules and casino policies; directing gamblers to gaming cashiers to collect winnings; working as part of a dealers team in games such like baccarat or craps; seating patrons at gaming

Professional Ethics

Treating Addiction

It is incumbent on anyone working within the gaming industry to be able to identify an individual with a gambling addiction. It can often be difficult to spot a compulsive gambler. For most people, gambling provides a harmless, entertaining diversion from the myopia of everyday life. Whether they are playing blackjack or keno, these folks are enjoying a time-honored activity by taking a chance on an unpredictable event in the hopes of winning based on correctly guessing the outcome. For other people, however, the act of placing the bet is a far different experience. What is normally a moment of elation or excitement is, for some gamblers, a moment of overwhelming compulsion—a moment in which these people are no longer in control of their behavior. These individuals cannot resist the impulse to gamble—they are compulsive gamblers.

Once a suspected compulsive gambler has been identified, he or she should no longer be allowed to participate in the establishment's gaming activities and should instead be advised of strategies for conquering their addiction. Many casinos have implemented training programs and responsible gaming tutorials and policies to assist their employees and patrons who have a gambling addiction.

tables; preparing collection reports for submission to gaming supervisors; monitoring gambling tables and supervising staff; and training new dealers.

Gaming Supervisor

The gaming supervisor (or pit boss) is both manager and arbiter. The pit boss will supervise several dealers operating several different games at the same time. The pit boss is expected to be an expert in the game(s) he or she oversees, and be able to offer rulings without hesitation. Ultimately, he or she is also there to make sure guests have a positive gaming experience.

The casino's profits increase when players play more hands or throw more dice, so it is therefore essential that the pit boss keeps the action moving. He or she rotates the dealers from game to game to facilitate effective play and preempts potential conflicts before they can become time-consuming problems.

The pit boss is the ultimate arbiter of the rules of the games he or she oversees. For any question a player has about a particular rule, the pit boss has the answer. If a player has a complaint about the way a game was played, it is the pit boss who handles the complaint. In the event of a dealer mistake (dropping a card, misplacing dice, overlooking a bet) the pit boss decides any and all corrections to play and pay. The pit boss also functions as an accountant. He or she must keep an eye on all of the bets in play at his or her tables while coordinating the flow of chips into the gaming area and cash going out. Everything must be accounted for, and all receipts must be signed and dated. In establishments where thousands of dollars change hands each minute, every penny of that money has to be accounted for by the pit bosses.

The pit boss is also part of the casino's security apparatus. Large amounts of money changes hands every minute and the pit bosses are making sure it all happens according the rules. For thousands of years, criminals have tried (and sometimes succeeded) at cheating casino games, and gaming establishments are always on the lookout for people who are seeking to gain an unfair advantage.

Pit bosses are also responsible for monitoring and managing "problem" guests. In a cut-throat environment where the fool and his money can be quite easily separated, the pit boss must be aware of circumstances when a player's unhappiness over a run of bad luck is starting to turn ugly. The pit bosses keep an eye on these problem players and will dispatch security personnel (both uniformed and undercover) to the area around the player while simultaneously minimizing the disruption to the gaming environment.

Finally, pit bosses also keep track of players' betting so that they can be properly rewarded for their betting habits. Casinos typically reward players who spend a lot of money with "comps" (typically free drinks or food, but in some case more lavish incentives such as free tickets or free hotel rooms), and it is the pit boss who doles out the comps. Like every other casino employee, it is ultimately the pit boss's job to keep the players happy.

Gaming Manager

The gaming manager, also known as the gaming supervisor or casino manager, oversees the operations and supervises the staff in an assigned area. He or she also interviews, hires, trains, schedules and evaluates the performance of the subordinate staff. The casino manager patrols the game areas, observing patrons and employees, to ensure that the casino's policies and procedures, as well as the rules of the individual games, are being followed. The gaming manager, therefore, must not only be familiar with the establishment's policies and procedures, he or she must also be thoroughly acquainted with the rules of the each game on the floor. The casino manager may be called upon to explain casino policies to customers, investigate and address complaints, and work to enhance the gambling experience of the casino guests. Casino management must be possessed of effective interpersonal and communication skills required for the constant interaction with guests and employees.

The gaming manager's job description typically includes most (if not all) of the following: circulating among the gaming tables to ensure that operations are being conducted properly and that dealers are following the house rules and that the players are not cheating the rules in any way; directing the pit bosses in the distribution of complimentary rooms, meals, and other free items that are dispensed to players according to their length of play and spending totals; directing workers in compiling summary sheets detailing wager amounts and payoffs, establishing house policies on gaming odds, extension of credit, and food and beverage service; maintaining familiarity with all games offered at a casino and the strategies employed in playing those games; coordinating extension of credit to players; monitoring staffing levels to ensure adequate staffing of games and tables and arranging staff rotations and breaks; preparing work schedules and table assignments and keeping attendance records; resolving customer complaints relating to problems such as payout errors and/or dealer errors; reviewing for accuracy all operational expenses, budget estimates, betting accounts and collection reports; setting and maintaining the bank and table limits for each game; tracking supplies of money to tables, and completing any required paperwork; explaining and interpreting house rules (such as game rules and betting limits) for players; interviewing and hiring employees; notifying subordinates of table vacancies; recording, collecting, and paying off bets and issuing receipts as necessary; supervising the ejection of suspected cheaters, including blackjack card counters and players utilizing illegal systems to shift the odds to their favor; and training new workers and evaluating their performance.

Chapter 4

Tips for Success

This chapter provides a roadmap for success in the hospitality industry. But first, it is important to note that achievement in any of the individual jobs within this industry is largely dependent upon a congenial and collaborative personality. In other words, if you want to succeed in the hospitality game, you have to work and play well with others.

To say that an individual's success within the hospitality industry is predicated upon him or her being "a people person" is the ultimate cliché. But in the world of hospitality, it is a literal truth. Hotels and restaurants are quintessential team operations whose employees must work in concert to maximize the comfort and satisfaction levels of their patrons—and doing so occasionally requires the subordination of such negative (and natural) feelings as frustration with fellow employees as well as the tolerance of disrespectful clientele. Your potential for success boils down to simple questions of temperament: Are you the kind of person who can emerge from a heated kitchen argument over misplaced gnocchi or watery gazpacho and still greet your table with a smile? Can you keep your cool when checking in an irate guest whose flight was delayed and whose luggage was lost? If not, then a hotel or restaurant may not be your ideal working environment. But if you are someone who can endure these types of worst case scenarios and still put on a happy face, you are ready to embark on an exciting and often rewarding career in the hospitality industry.

There are two basic paths you can follow to find work and move up in the hospitality industry. The first is to obtain outside schooling or training, after which you will try to secure employment. The second is to jump directly into a profession at a lower level and learn the business from the ground up.

Formal Training versus Learning on the Job

With the exception of bartending classes, jobs in the hospitality industry for which outside schooling is available tend to be restricted to hotel management and "back of house" restaurant work. Hotel management and culinary schools generally offer degree programs and require a substantial investment of time and money. Bartending classes, by contrast, typically necessitate a smaller financial commitment and can be completed much more quickly.

Hotel Management School

By providing the skills, knowledge, and hands-on training required for professional development, hotel management training is an invaluable asset for success in the resort and hospitality industry. Hotel management schools offer specialized training for managerial positions in this highly competitive industry. A hotel management degree program typically includes courses in accounting, service management, economics, business relations and finance, marketing and sales, communications, employee relations, and human resources. Hotel management education courses are available in two categories: (1) food service and banquet services, and (2) resort, hotel, and motel management. Students at hotel management colleges benefit from the opportunity to collaborate with other students on various projects. Because customer service

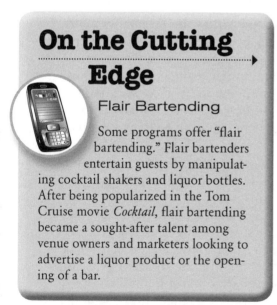

On the Cutting Edge

Flair Bartending

Some programs offer "flair bartending." Flair bartenders entertain guests by manipulating cocktail shakers and liquor bottles. After being popularized in the Tom Cruise movie *Cocktail*, flair bartending became a sought-after talent among venue owners and marketers looking to advertise a liquor product or the opening of a bar.

and employee relations are of such paramount importance, students are also educated in key communication skills,

The single greatest advantage of enrolling in a hotel school is the opportunity to expedite the path to a very lucrative career. Most graduates of hotel management schools find jobs with a gross annual pay of up to $60,000 immediately after graduation. And they often ascend more quickly to varied positions such as catering manager, human resources manager, or even business development assistant.

Learning on the Job—Hotel Management

At one time, aspiring hotel managers began their careers at the reception desk or in other low-level positions and then worked their way up. Over time, as the duties of hotel managers have expanded, this avenue of advancement has become less common; today, a hotel management degree is considered *de rigueur*. However, it is still *possible* to move up the food chain, most frequently from the desk clerk or concierge positions. It is worth noting that a lack of formal education can put you at an initial disadvantage in comparison to your competitors. To compensate, you will need to pay especially close attention to details and instructions and always show willingness to learn and eagerness to go the extra mile.

Most hotel desk clerks go through an orientation period, during which they receive on the job training. An orientation provides an overview of the specific job duties as well as background about the establishment itself, such as the arrangement of guest rooms, availability of services, location of nearby restaurants and stores, and so on.

Larger hotel chains generally offer greater opportunities for advancement than their smaller, independently-owned-and-operated competitors. These large chains often have career "ladder programs," and many afford desk clerks the opportunity to participate in management training programs.

Culinary School

Culinary arts schools are specialized institutions that focus on the art, design, and science of food preparation. All schools offer a curriculum that results in certification, either in the form a degree (for example, an associate's or bachelor's degree in food and nutrition) or certification that indicates a certain level of competency.

Many culinary institutions are associated with restaurants, allowing students the opportunity to gain hands-on experience. Some schools choose to have independent culinary federations and organizations award certifications to their students. Newer institutions even now offer online courses so students can work while gaining certification.

Choosing a culinary school should be based in large part, but certainly not entirely, on the following criteria:

→ Tuition—The cost of education is a major factor, especially when taking into account the state of the economy and the reality that entry-level jobs usually come with entry-level wages. The good news is that financial aid is often available.

→ Location—Can you relocate? Or must you stay close to home? If you want to stay in your area, your choice of schools may be more limited. Willingness to relocate offers a greater diversity of opportunity.

→ Program Length—Do you want to get through a training program before entering the workforce as quickly as possible? Or are you looking to earn a degree (such as an associate's or bachelor's) that will serve as a foundation for more advanced education? Some certificate programs may be only a few weeks of intensive training. At the other end of the spectrum, a bachelor's degree is generally a four-year program that provides a complete and well-rounded education.

→ Career Placement Services—Does the school you are interested in have career placement services or externship opportunities? When speaking with admissions counselors, find out if they have placement statistics on previous graduates.

Learning on the Job—Back of the House Restaurant Jobs

Without a formal education, the only way to rise within the world of food-preparation is by starting at the very bottom. Learning the business by working from the bottom up gives an aspiring chef actual hands-on experience that is not readily available at cooking school.

Real world experience is sometimes more respected than the kind of theoretical knowledge that a student fresh out of culinary school brings to the table. While a restaurant owner may be impressed by a culinary degree, it will not tell him or her whether you have what it takes to negotiate the stressful kitchen environment. All of this said, learning on the job does carry with it tremendous disadvantages. In a restaurant kitchen, the primary objective is to prepare quality dishes to the customer's satisfaction, and the head chef will not have time to explain to you how a dish is made, or the history and culture that fostered it. These are the things one learns in culinary school. So you will have to study these things on your own and try to couple your outside learning with what you observe on a day-to-day basis.

Bartending School

Bartending schools generally require a minimum of training hours for completion of their individual programs, which can be accumulated on a full- or part-time basis. Most schools require students be at least 18 years of age, but some insist on a minimum age of 21. Obtaining a bartending license is the initial goal for completing a successful bartending course—though using that certification to obtain employment is, of course, the larger objective. Most schools offer courses that cover skills such as: bar set-up, bar equipment and utensils, opening and closing procedures, free pouring, drink recipes and preparation, speed drills, wine, beer and spirit knowledge, register training, alcohol awareness programs, catering and private parties and interviewing and job hunting skills.

Knowledge about fine wines and champagne is a must for a good bartender, as is familiarity with spirits and liquor (and the mixing of those substances). Bartending schools also acquaint students with the fermentation of lagers and ales. Better bartending schools have keg tap systems where students learn to properly tap a keg and pour beer. Many schools offer a chance to meet people from prominent spirit production companies.

Bartending schools sometimes offer alcohol awareness certifications. These programs teach acceptable standards for serving alcoholic beverages. Typically covered are topics such as intervention strategies for handling difficult situations, third-party liquor liability laws, and how to avoid lawsuits. Some states require certification in alcohol awareness training in order for a bartender to obtain his or her license. In addition, many bartending schools offer students the opportunity to guest bartend at local bars where they can gain invaluable, hands-on experience.

Learning on the Job—Bartending

Though it can be difficult to land a bartending job without some degree of formal training, it is possible to work your way up to the position by beginning as a barback. A barback position is typically an entry-level job where you will learn the basics of setup, breakdown, and keeping the bartender stocked with everything he or she needs. A hard-working barback in a good bar can make decent money— and the job will provide real-world experience that can ultimately lead to a bartending position.

Service Academies

While there are myriad distinguished culinary schools around the country, where do restaurant waiters and servers most frequently learn their craft? Most of them learn by experience and are taught by the various establishments by whom they are employed. All newly hired employees receive some training from their employer. For example, they learn safe food-handling procedures and sanitation practices. Some employers, particularly those in fast-food restaurants, teach new workers by using self-study programs, on-line programs, audiovisual presentations, and instructional booklets that explain food preparation and service skills.

But most food- and beverage-serving workers acquire their skills through observation of their more-experienced co-workers. Prospective waiters can also hone their skills by attending classes offered by vocational schools or restaurant associations. Also, some full-service restaurants offer new employees formalized classroom training augmented by on-the-job work experience. These training programs help to familiarize the employee with the restaurant and the other staff members, instill proper service technique, and promote the importance of teamwork. Prospective waiters with no restaurant experience should seek out restaurants with training programs. Corporate-owned chain restaurants are more likely offer such programs. From there, servers with more lofty career goals can take this new experience with them and seek employment at more-esteemed establishments.

Finding a Job in the Hospitality Industry

As with any industry, the best and most expedient method for finding a job in a restaurant or hotel is through connections. While the cliché "It's not what you know, it's *who* you know" isn't exactly true (after all, at the end of the day you may not need to know exactly what you are doing to succeed in *any* job), having a connection to help you to get your foot in the door can be as invaluable as any sterling résumé or Ivy League diploma.

For the job seeker, one distinct advantage that the hospitality industry holds over many others lies in its ubiquity. This is not the case with most other fields. You could go your whole life without ever meeting a corporate executive or computer programmer, but two of our most basic needs are food and shelter. As such, the hospitality industry plays an important role in almost everyone's daily life. Most people know someone who is a "regular" at a restaurant or hotel (if they are not regulars themselves). Ask a friend or family member who frequents an establishment to introduce you to a manager or owner who knows them. Regulars are the lifeblood of any business within the service industry, and so a manager or owner's desire to keep a repeat customer happy will often render them receptive to your inquiries.

Unfortunately, it is all too often the case that one must "pound the pavement" in order to find work. While the old-school methods of finding employment (such as job boards and classified advertisements) still exist, they have been largely usurped by the technical advancements of the information age. Accordingly, many of the Web sites listed in Chapter 6 feature postings for jobs in the hospitality industry. In addition to those hospitality-specific sites, you might also consider more-traditional career-assistance sites, such as Monster.com, Careerbuilder.com, Craigslist, and Hot Jobs.

Acing the Interview

No matter how impressive your education or credentials, if you cannot impress a prospective employer with your winning personality and professional demeanor, your chances for getting a job offer are slim. The following tips will help you to maximize your chances of securing employment in the hospitality industry. Some of this advice may seem obvious, while some may surprise you. Either way, by following these basic rules you are sure to be in the right frame of mind for a successful interview.

➡ Be on time—Try to arrive for your interview about 15 minutes early. This will give you a buffer in case of an unexpected travel delay.

➡ Be polite—Recognize that you are being watched. From the moment you arrive, the interview has begun (even if interviewer is not present).

➡ Do your homework—If you arrive knowing the executive chef's name and the restaurant's signature dishes and ingredients, you will seem both studious and diligent. Preparation shows enthusiasm, and is certain to impress your interviewer.

➡ Be confident—A firm handshake, poise, and a friendly demeanor will get an employer's attention before you even open your mouth.

➡ Look sharp—Your manner of dress should be consistent with the position you seek. Always err on the side of overdressing. It goes without saying that you should be freshly groomed, well coiffed, and your clothes should be cleaned and pressed.

➡ Relax—Remember to breathe and collect your thoughts before answering questions. Don't rush. And don't be afraid to ask for clarification if you need it.

➡ Take your cues from the interviewer—If a potential employer is very businesslike, your demeanor should also be entirely professional. If, by contrast, he or she is more conversational, your responses can be a bit more relaxed.

➡ Do not talk about money—Unless the interviewer mentions it, do not bring it up. It is a good idea to be prepared for a question about your salary requirements, but try to forestall a compensation discussion until you have been made an offer.

➡ Ask questions—At the conclusion of most job interviews, you will often be given a chance to ask questions. Be sure to ask at least one question, or you may seem disinterested.

➡ Follow up—Ask for contact information from each person with whom you interview. Later, write a short e-mail to each interviewer thanking them for the opportunity, and send it out within a day. This immediate follow-up will demonstrate your seriousness and professionalism.

Succeeding in the Hospitality World

The following section offers critical tips and strategies to help you get ahead within the industry's various jobs.

Moving Up the Ranks—Hotels

Once you have secured a low-level position within a hotel, begin thinking about your next move up. Start working toward your goal from day one. A good first step is to seek certification(s). The American Hotel and Lodging Educational Institute offers many certifications for professionals working in hotel and hospitality jobs, ranging from Certified Hotel Administrator (CHA) to Certified Gaming Supervisor (CGS) to Certified Hospitality Trainer (CHT). While these certifications are not required for all positions, they will expand your knowledge and demonstrate your commitment to the hospitality industry.

Always bear in mind that serving the guests should be your number one priority. If a guest asks you a question for which you do not have an answer, find someone to assist him or her. All hospitality and hotel jobs are ultimately customer service-oriented and therefore all employees need to make pleasing guests their main concern. In the hotel industry, frequent and unexpected situations arise that require employees to perform outside of their job descriptions. Always volunteer to assist in these circumstances and you will gain the respect of your superiors. If your manager can count on you in a pinch, your name will be at the top of the list when new job opportunities become available

Most importantly, and whenever possible, present yourself as a problem-solver. The ability to analyze a situation and devise a solution is an indicator of professional development. If, for example, you have an issue with a hotel guest that requires managerial attention, offer your manager a possible solution. This will demonstrate your ability to think on your feet and announce your potential for greater responsibility.

Hotel Managers

Education and experience have given you the basic knowledge of what the business end of your hotel requires but, at the end of the day, effective and considerate staff management is the most crucial of the hotel manager's responsibilities. If you treat your staff with dignity and respect, they will in turn treat your guests the same way and will take pride in their work. Quality service is what customers expect, so caring for your employees will ensure that your customers are well taken care of. Happy employees provide quality in their work. A staff that feels valued and appreciated will invariably outperform one that feels marginalized.

The following tips will help you to properly care for your employees' needs and, by extension, those of your guests.

1. Be visible. Employees should feel connected to their managers, and you cannot create this connection with someone who is always locked away in his or her office. By simply being present you will break down the perceived barriers between manager and staff.

2. Act decisively and quickly. Never postpone important discussions, meetings, or, when necessary, the termination of an employee. The longer you allow a problem to fester, the greater the opportunity for that problem to infect other areas of the operation.

3. Hire well. Employees who are not suited to their job will inevitably let you down and will ferment dissatisfaction with your judgment among the staff.

4. Challenge your employees. Staff members will be more productive when they are tested and must therefore rise to the occasion. Encourage friendly competition and reward those who exceed expectations.

5. Never condescend. As a general manager, you must realize that your success results directly from the success of your employees and the way they interact with customers. Praise your employees when business is good in order to demonstrate your dependence on them.

6. Focus on communication. It is crucial that you listen and communicate effectively with employees and customers alike so as to alleviate problems as quickly as possible.

7. Pay attention. Know all of the details that go into the daily operation of the hotel. An effective manager knows each employee's responsibilities down to the smallest detail, and can advise any employee on effective techniques for improving the performance of any task.

8. Be respectful. When possible, try to reprimand in private and praise in public. Pointing out an employee's mistakes in front of his or her co-workers is belittling, while congratulating them publicly will make them feel proud.

Moving Up the Ranks—Restaurants

Front of house positions available to those without any prior restaurant experience are typically those of busser and host/hostess. Restaurants usually train the new employees in these roles, which provide an excellent opportunity to gain familiarity with the restaurant world (which, as anyone who has ever worked in it will attest, is unique unto itself).

Your move to the next rung on the ladder—that of server—will depend largely on your job performance as busser. Communication is also important. Let your manager know that you are interested in becoming a server, and let him or her know that you are willing to shadow a server during your open shifts. You should also volunteer to fill in if a server should happen to call in sick. One other advantage you have is that restaurants prefer to promote from within.

A job as a server will give you ample opportunity to practice your customer service skills—which will, in turn, ultimately make you a better restaurant manager. You will also have a chance to gain a good understanding of what it takes for the front-of-the-house operations to run smoothly.

Waiters

Waiting tables is a highly stressful, physically demanding, and emotionally exhausting occupation. Without question, it is not for the faint of heart. As a waiter, you are responsible for every need of every patron seated in your station—and sometimes you will discover that every one of them seems to require your attention at exactly the same moment. You will find yourself confronted constantly by demanding guests, impatient chefs, unsympathetic managers, and incompetent subordinates.

The following strategies will help to maximize your job performance and ensure that you provide the best possible service for your guests. Follow these tips and you will be doubly rewarded (earning the approval of your manager as well as a generous gratuity from your customer).

1. Be on time. Whenever possible, arrive at 10 minutes ahead of your scheduled shift.

2. Be presentable. Make sure you are well-groomed and your clothes are clean and wrinkle-free. Your hair should be neat and washed, your nails clean, your uniform/ clothes clean and modest. Minimize makeup and perfume, particularly the latter since you do not want your scent to overpower that of the cuisine.

3. Approach each table with a warm smile and a friendly greeting. Introduce yourself. Establish eye contact, but do not stare. Be friendly and personable as you take their drink orders.

4. If there are children at the table, take their drink orders first, followed by ladies and then gentleman all following the left to right order. This is typically the time when you will present the specials. Speak slowly and explain each dish thoroughly. Try (even though you will have the specials memorized) to avoid sounding robotic and rattling them off in a lackluster monotone. Just because you have repeated the specials ten times, remember that this is the first time your guests are hearing them.

5. After drinks are served, ask your guests if they have any questions about the menu. If they are ready, take their orders clockwise from the guest seated to your left.

6. Never bring one guest's food without bringing everyone else's—unless they have specifically asked you to do so. (This might occur when someone in a party must leave before the others). If a circumstance arises in which one order is taking longer than the rest, explain the situation to the table and ask how they want you to handle it.

7. Be attentive, but not pushy. Do not hover over a table. If you remain alert and vigilant when you are on the floor, most customers will make eye contact to signal you. When their meals are eaten and conversation starts to run dry, diners will inevitably start looking around the restaurant. This is a clear sign that it is time to clear the plates and offer desserts or the check.

8. Clear plates once it is obvious the customer is ready for them to be removed.

Keeping
in Touch

Termination Communication

Terminating an employee is never a pleasant experience, but at some point it is something anyone working in a managerial capacity must deal with. The key to successfully conducting a termination is proper communication. Always try to be succinct and be sure to have at your fingertips the relevant facts that justify the firing. The following tips will further assist you in navigating this potentially treacherous process.

- Always provide concrete examples of poor job performance. Failure to do so could be grounds for a wrongful-termination lawsuit.

- Detail the benefits, severance pay, and unused vacation time to which the employee is entitled, if any.

- Stay on point and try to limit the conversation to 10 minutes or less.

- If the employee has access to any sensitive information or computer files, change passwords and codes after the employee is terminated.

- Do not be swayed by tears and begging from employees, or else word will get around that you lack the intestinal fortitude to handle the more unpleasant aspects of your job.

- Never allow yourself to be drawn into a shouting match with the employee.

- After the firing, gather the remaining staff members together and explain to them what's happened and why. Explain how the firing will affect them, the responsibilities that will be shifted, and your plan for hiring a replacement.

- If you are conducting an exit interview, focus on facts that led to the dismissal, not on the individual's personal shortcoming. When possible, have the exit interview in private and at the end of a shift.

- If you have any reason to believe the terminated employee could turn violent, make arrangements to have security personnel on the premises.

- Treat the employee respectfully. Never publicly embarrass him or her.

9. Before bringing plates from the next course to a table, always completely clear the plates from the previous course. Politely inquire as to whether a guest is finished before clearing a plate.

10. After serving the main course, ask the guests if you can bring them anything else and give them a moment for consideration. Check back with the table a few minutes later to be sure that everything is to their satisfaction.

11. Once the main course is cleared, ask if your guests would like to see the dessert menu. If not, and they are finished with their meal, promptly give them their bill and politely bid them good night. Leave the check in the middle of the table, face down, unless one of the patrons has made it clear to you that he or she will be paying.

12. Take their payment promptly. If they pay with cash, always ask if they want change.

13. When you return with change or a credit card receipt, thank them for their patronage and bid them goodnight. Be careful not to seem as though you are rushing them out the door. Remember that some guests like to linger at their table after dinner.

In addition to these useful strategies, here are some useful tricks of the trade that will help you to improve your overall job performance (leading to an increase in both your tips and your chances for promotion):

1. Repeat orders back to customers after you take them. This will help to double check for mistakes and simultaneously demonstrate your professionalism.

2. Be aware of proper table service technique. Always serve from the left and remove from the right. This knowledge is critical to job performance in an upscale restaurant, but is certainly useful in any circumstance.

3. Know how to properly set a table. Though there are some general rules (for example, fork on the left, knife on the right) many restaurants have specific criteria for how they want their tables set.

4. Clear tables quickly and quietly, minimizing disturbance to the diners at neighboring tables.

5. Memorize the menu ASAP and thoroughly familiarize yourself with its dishes and their ingredients.

6. Assist your fellow waiters when you have time. Not only does this demonstrate good manners, but they will also be that much more likely to help you when *you* are slammed. Cooperation between coworkers is crucial to job performance.

7. Be friendly, but not too chatty. This fine line may vary depending on the establishment and the customer, but it is a good rule of thumb to let the customer dictate just how conversational your relationship will be.

8. Never promise a customer you will do something and then neglect to do it—and *never* make a promise upon which you cannot deliver.

9. If called upon to answer the phone, speak clearly and be sure you understand what a customer needs. Do your best to serve his or her needs, or find someone who can do so.

10. If there is a break in the action and you are talking with co-workers, be sure to face your tables so you can see if anyone needs anything. Customers can grow annoyed if they are looking for service only to find you standing with your back turned and chatting with your friends.

11. Always have a spare shirt with you, because spills in a restaurant are nothing if not inevitable.

12. When fielding customer complaints, do not try to pass the buck to the cooks, hostess, or anyone else for that matter. Apologize and work to resolve the problem. (Handling difficult customers is dealt with in greater detail later in the chapter.)

13. Never complain to customers or coworkers. Quite simply, no one wants to hear it. Check your problems at the door.

14. Be polite at all times. Say "sir" when addressing a man and "ma'am" when addressing a woman.

15. Talk to the kids. If they are being loud or obnoxious, offer to bring them crayons or something else to keep them busy. The parents will be grateful for your assistance.

16. Be friendly with the bussers. If you treat them with respect, they will help you out more and make your life infinitely easier.

Bartenders

If you have been hired as a bartender, it is likely that you know how to make drinks as well as a bar's basic rules of service. The following tips and strategies are offered for those not satisfied with being merely "good" bartenders. By employing these rules, you will distinguish yourself from the crowd and earn a reputation for superior customer service (and better gratuities).

1. Keep it clean—As much as possible, keep your bar surface spotless. Maintaining an immaculate bar demonstrates a general concern for performance and professionalism that will be appreciated by both your guests and employers.

2. Finish strong—Make sure that you properly garnish your cocktails. If you are unsure as to which garnish is appropriate, consult a bartending book. Once again, this kind of attention to detail will assure you a high performance rating.

3. Be honest—If you do not know how to make a particular cocktail, never pretend to a customer that you do. Look it up in the bar manual (or ask a co-worker) in order to ensure correct preparation.

4. Be fresh—Make sure to use fresh garnishes. Your customers will not notice how well you have mixed their cocktail if you finish it with a wilted lemon wedge or a craggy olive. Cut fresh fruit whenever you have a free moment and always keep your garnishes chilled.

5. Know your customers—Remember the names of your regular customers and their drinks of choice. When greeting a returning guest, offer his or her usual cocktail. Also, try to recall if they like their drink garnished in a particular way (or any other personally idiosyncratic preferences).

6. Give recommendations—Never assume that a patron wants a "well" drink because he or she does not name a specific brand. Ask for a favorite brand, and recommend one if he or she does not have one. This technique (known as "up selling") is invaluable to increasing your sales (and, again, your tips!).

7. Be neat—Wear clean clothing and make certain that your uniform is properly clean and pressed. Make sure you are

well-groomed and clean-shaven, and that your hands are impeccably clean at all times.

Restaurant Managers

To succeed as a restaurant manager, you must possess a combination of skills that enable the effective supervision of an ever-changing and inevitably chaotic environment.

The most important of these skills are leadership and effective management. If someone on the floor (or in the kitchen) has a problem, a manager must step in, analyze the situation, and then find an expeditious solution. Other responsibilities that fall under the manager's purview (scheduling, billing, and inventory, for example) are, of course, also important. But they are generally administrative in nature. A good manager is distinguished from a mediocre one by virtue of his or her people skills, as evidenced by how well he or she masters the following:

1. Human resources skills—Employee turnover is very high in the restaurant business, so an effective manager should always be recruiting (either to fill newly open spots or to upgrade the existing personnel). A restaurant manager should be personally involved in new-employee training to ensure that all of his or her team members have the skills needed to do their jobs. And, of course, good managers must do their best to keep their staff motivated and happy so that they will not want to find work elsewhere.

2. Motivation—Keeping employees motivated and happy boils down to leadership. Managing a restaurant is more than just filling the staff roles and posting a schedule. Good restaurant managers take it upon themselves to acquaint themselves with each employees' strengths, weaknesses, and levels of commitment and then challenges each to improve in any area of noticeable deficiency.

3. Comprehensive knowledge—A chef will not respect a restaurant manager if he or she does not know what ingredients are in the food, and the waitresses and hostesses will not respect a restaurant manager if he or she does not have a firm grasp of the principles of good services. It is

INTERVIEW

What It Takes to Make It in the Hospitality Industry

Patrick Byrne,
Owner, O'Hanlon's Bar and The Vig Bar, New York, New York

How long have you worked in the restaurant business? How did your personal career path evolve?
I started tending bar during college to help pay my bills. After college I decided to work tending bar in order to save cash to travel. I traveled for a while, spent all my money, and found myself bartending again! After bartending and saving for four more years, I decided to open my own place with some friends. It was never my intention or goal to get into the industry. I went to college for marketing and management but never found myself drawn to an office or nine-to-five lifestyle, nor did I ever think I would own two bars in Manhattan.

What tips for success might you offer a young person just starting out in the food service industry? What does it take to make it? And on the contrary, what words of caution might you have?
Be prepared to do anything at any time. And because many of the jobs in the industry do not require vast experience, it's important to highlight yourself as an enthusiastic member of the staff. The phrase, "that's not my job" is certainly not a welcome one in an industry where your replacement's résumé is in the manager's drawer. Making yourself useful beyond your job description will get you noticed and rapidly increase your chances of advancement.

What are the most important qualities a person needs to succeed in your line of work?
1. Patience. Many of the first jobs you hold in the hospitality in-dustry are at the bottom rung. No matter where you work there is always a pecking order and new staff members tend to get the less desirable shifts where they make less money and often

crucial for a restaurant manager to be extensively familiar with every aspect of operation of the restaurant, and he or she must be able to step into any role should the need arise.

work longer hours. This form of "apprenticeship" is essentially unavoidable. However, due to a high rate of staff turnover in the industry, a patient and enthusiastic member of staff will always be high on the list for better shifts.

2. High Energy. The nature of the business is such that you are always performing, so to speak. You are at a job that you are doing day in and day out but each customer is coming in with his or her own expectations of a certain experience in mind. It's your job to create that experience, tailoring it for each individual customer. Anyone can serve a beer or take a food order but the person who does it with a little extra effort and with the customer's interest in mind will always succeed. The benefits of satisfied customers are many—and for the servers means better tips! But in the long run, a really happy customer is far more important than that 20 percent tip. If he or she is happy, he or she will come back repeatedly, creating many 20 percents for you and more business for your establishment. Staff that brings high energy and sincere service to work every day is invaluable to any establishment.

3. Honesty. Honesty is of paramount importance. Even with the high volume of credit cards today, there is still a lot of cash involved in the hospitality industry. It's important that people know they can trust you.

4. Confidence. Being confident, as in any industry, is not only the easiest way in the door but it's also essential for advancement. Like I said, bartenders, waitstaff, and managers in this industry are always performing; doing so confidently puts you ahead!

How important do you consider formal/academic training for someone interested in a career in bars?
Personally, I don't think formal training is necessary. Even at the highest levels of the industry you hear stories of people starting as bus boys and working their way up to general manager positions. This is an industry where on-the-job training is constant and hard work and loyalty are rewarded. Formal training might help you skip a few rungs of the ladder—but many a hospitality graduate has been humbled mopping out bathrooms!

4. Multitasking—If there is one thing you can count on during any restaurant shift, it is that all problems will occur at the same time. (While this may be an exaggeration, it is more common than not!) The best managers are those

Professional
Ethics

When to Stop Serving

It is your first day at your new bartending job, and you notice that one of your patrons is becoming slightly drunk. He is slurring his words and speaking a bit too loudly. But he is not being obnoxious or falling off his stool. A situation like this raises the question: how do you know when it is time to cut someone off?

One of the most important issues facing anyone who serves alcohol is knowing when to stop serving a patron before he or she is overly intoxicated. This is especially important because restaurants or bars (or even bartenders themselves) can be held legally responsible for a drunken driving accident if it is proven that the establishment served alcohol to a visibly intoxicated individual.

Many states currently have "Dram Shop laws," which state that drinking establishments can be held liable in civil court if it is demonstrated that they served alcohol to a minor or an already-inebriated patron. What this means, essentially, is that if someone is seriously injured (or killed) as the result of your patron having driven when intoxicated, the victim or the victim's family can sue your bar or restaurant.

It is therefore essential for any bartender to become skilled at judging how intoxicated customers are getting and whether or not they need to be cut off. To assist service employees in recognizing the signs of over-intoxication, many states offer alcohol awareness classes. In New York, for example, the State Liquor Authority provides training programs that teach bar and restaurant employees how to identify intoxicated patrons and methods for intervening when the patron has reached his or her limit. Although these training programs are not legally required, training courses like ATAP (Alcohol Training Awareness Program) and TIPS (Training for Intervention Procedures) are recognized by the state as legitimate courses.

In New York, authorized courses can be used as defenses in civil cases. So if a bar or restaurant (or bartender) is sued for damages resulting from a DWI accident, demonstrating that employees have attended certain courses can potentially absolve the establishment of blame.

who can act quickly, effectively prioritizing the solutions to multiple issues while still finding time to thank the customers on their way out the door.

5. Grace under pressure—Chaos ensues in most restaurants at some point during a busy shift, and it is up to the manager to exude tranquility. Emotions tend to run high and tempers often flare when rush begins, and it is the manager's job to provide a steady, calming influence to his or her employees.

6. Energy—The restaurant life is a demanding one. An effective manager will persevere through long periods of activity while maintaining poise and serving as an example to subordinates.

Handling Difficult Guests, Coworkers, and Bosses

You already know that, even in restaurants, life is not a bowl of cherries. On the contrary, and even in the best-kept kitchens, it can be more like a bowl of sour milk. Needless to say, there are occasions in any job when one must deal with hostile or generally unpleasant people. For the hospitality worker eager to be service-oriented, these can be the biggest challenges. The following are some quick tips that will help you to effectively diffuse tense situations and foster more productive relationships in the service industry.

Guests

Dealing with difficult customers is a fact of life in the hospitality game. Negative personalities can precipitate employee burnout and low staff morale. However, if handled correctly, difficult customers can usually be appeased and the tense circumstances they create defused. Your first order of business is to simply hear them out. *This step is vital.* Let the customer drain some of his or her emotion and anger. Do not interrupt them, but let your body language indicate that you are listening intently. It is important to express an understanding of how they feel, even if you do not agree with them. Having done this, the next step is to try to solve the problem. Tell the customer what you intend to do to rectify the situation, and try to make him or her feel good about the solution. This should provide at least temporary satisfaction. (It may also serve to bring them back to your establishment again in the future.)

Coworkers

Before deciding how to deal with difficult coworkers, first reflect on the *circumstances* of the difficulties. A small conflict may be one that you can handle on your own, but more serious problems may call for more drastic action. In the case of smaller issues, one of the first things you should do is to speak privately with the difficult coworker. Be as forthright, gracious, and magnanimous as possible—since sporting an attitude will likely only incite more tension. Try to come up with a solution before the meeting. If you are frustrated with a coworker who never seems to complete his or her work in a timely manner, you may consider offering time-management

Problem
Solving

Handling Tension

Although occasional employee conflict is unavoidable, managers must not allow their workplace to lapse into the culture of conflict that is the scourge of poorly run restaurants. Such conflict becomes ingrained because of poor resolution policies and managerial practices. Ongoing and unchecked discord will inevitably lead to the very circumstances managers want to avoid: unnecessary employee turnover and the kinds of distraction that take the focus off customer service.

For restaurants, a common flashpoint for trouble is tension between the front and back of house. Accordingly, managers need to ensure that both groups work together and that a harmonious atmosphere exists (which is conducive to good customer service). Remember that employees often bring their personal issues to work with them, and in busy restaurants they sometimes forget to be professional, becoming embroiled in conflicts with other workers. It is the manager's job to keep his or her staff focused on the matters at hand and to stamp out any flames of disquiet as soon as they appear.

Employee conflicts are sometimes based on deeper and more-disturbing issues such as sexual harassment or racial bias. A manager must clearly establish that such behaviors will not be tolerated under any circumstances.

tips. If you are dealing with an individual who is simply obnoxious, it is better to cite specific examples rather than simply decry his or her personality.

In the case of more serious issues, it may not always be prudent to arrange a one-on-one meeting. For instance, if you feel that you are being harassed—sexually or otherwise—you may want to refrain from speaking alone with the "offender." Consider recruiting the company of your supervisor for such loaded confrontations in an effort to keep things as civil as possible.

Bosses

One of the most challenging workplace scenarios is learning to get along with a superior who seems to be, in one way or another, making your job difficult for you. Since you are in the subordinate position, it will be difficult (perhaps even impossible) to change his or her attitude through direct confrontation. You must therefore try to find another way to deal with the situation—such as learning to *manage* your manager.

If your boss has a difficult management style, respond with professionalism. If your boss insults you or puts you down, calmly let him or her know that this makes you uncomfortable. If you explain your point of view rationally, your boss will be much more likely to consider your point of view. Always remember that you *do* work for your boss, so as long as what the boss is asking for is legal, then it is technically your job to do what your boss requests (no matter how imbecilic or unnecessary it may seem to you).

Getting the Promotion

In any industry, moving up through the ranks is achieved through a combination of performance and attitude. The world of hospitality is no different. The key to securing a promotion lies in a superlative work ethic and an organized, directed approach.

Start by visualizing where you would like to be in your career and the path you will need to take to accomplish your goal. Decide where you would like to be in the next six months, the next year, the next five years, and so on—and figure out what it will take for you to get there. Let your superiors know your career goals. They are often aware of opportunities before anyone else. By gaining their support in your career goals, they can help you achieve them.

One of the surest methods for impressing one's superiors is displaying exceptional diligence and mastery of your current position. Take an active leadership role that lets you shine and shows your superiors that you can deal with extra responsibility. You will not only gain valuable experience by learning new things, but you will have the opportunity to get your hard work noticed. By staying in touch with those in your work environment, you can gain valuable access to information about upcoming promotions, trends in your industry, and growth within the company. Encourage your superiors to give you extra projects or tasks that will help you work towards your goal. Ask them what it takes to achieve the promotion you are looking for and then work at acquiring those skills.

Getting a promotion is about working hard and making sure the right people notice. By planning, networking, and communicating, you can facilitate this process.

Eight Tips for Getting Started as an Entrepreneur

Unlike most industries, there exists within the hospitality industry the very real opportunity for opening your own establishment. Bars and restaurants, in particular, have start-up costs that are within reach of the would-be small business owner.

Few career opportunities are as exciting as the prospect of owning your own bar or restaurant. Such establishments can be home away from home for your best customers, and you are the king or queen of their castles.

Owning your own bar or restaurant means long hours, giving up vacations and weekends, and sometimes dealing with obnoxious customers. But if you have a clear vision, do your homework, and learn the ins and outs of the business, the opportunity can translate into a personally rewarding and financially successful enterprise. Here is how to get started:

1. Decide what kind of bar or restaurant you want to open. Bars vary from neighborhood pubs to sports bars to specialty bars (such as martini bars). Restaurant range from corner bistros to large, fine-dining establishments. (You could also opt to open a wine bar or a club with dancing or live entertainment.)

2. Check out the general demographic of your establishment's proposed location. Be sure to select a neighborhood that is conducive to your plan.

3. Research the latest in the bar and restaurant business. Liquor and food wholesalers keep records of how their product lines fit the local market.

4. Find out about other places in the area of your proposed location. Peruse local Web sites and periodicals to learn where people go, what is hot, what works—and, most importantly, what does not.

5. Scout the perfect location. Target a certain neighborhood or part of town, and find a setting that is convenient with lots of exposure and foot traffic.

6. Choose a name for your restaurant or bar. A name is more important than most people realize. Having a memorable name can help to fix your place in the minds of the public. Be sure to pick a name that supports your customer's expectations.

7 Write a business plan. Put a business plan together that challenges you and brings home the reality of every-thing involved in running a bar. Project the costs for build-up and opening expenses, fixtures, furniture, and equipment.

8 Consider investors. Speak with an investment broker once you have a solid business plan. You may be eligible for a small business loan.

Chapter 5

Talk Like a Pro

Use this glossary to help familiarize yourself with the various terms and expressions of the hospitality industry. Doing so will save you a great deal of confusion and potential embarrassment during your first days on the job, as well as allow you the time to focus on the many other skills you will need to learn.

ABA American Bus Association. The ABA represents approximately 1,000 motorcoach and tour companies in the United States and Canada.

all day Total number of any dish needed, considering all orders. For example: "I have three salmon on the first check and two salmon on the second check. I need five all day."

American Plan (AP) Room rate which includes service of three meals (breakfast, lunch, and dinner).

apartment hotel Rooms with cooking facilities.

aperitif Cocktail designed to cleanse the palette before a meal.

appetizer A smaller dish that precedes the main course designed to open the appetite (or reduce it).

attendance building A marketing promotion created to boost attendance at conventions, trade shows, meetings, and so on.

attractions Travel industry term referring to local sites with visitor appeal such as museums, historic sites, performing arts venues, and theme parks.

available rooms (suites, beds) The number of rooms available for guests on a daily basis, not including those used for purposes other than guest occupancy.

average daily rate (ADR)   Total room revenue for a length of time (day, month, year-to-date), divided by the number of rooms occupied for the same period.

AVHRM   Association of Vacation Home Rental Managers.

back of house   Areas without customer contact. In a restaurant, this refers to the kitchen, dishwashing area, and wait station (which are located in the back of the house and are thus restricted to kitchen and wait staff). At a hotel, this refers to support and service areas usually not seen by guests.

back-ordered   An item not in stock that can be shipped at a later date.

barback   A bartender's assistant whose job includes running glasses through the dishwasher, as well as stocking the coolers and liquor bottles.

bed and breakfast (B&B)   Establishment whose room rate includes breakfast.

bed tax (Transient Occupancy Tax or TOT)   A city or county tax added to the price of a hotel room.

bev nap   A small square paper napkin on which beverages rest.

block   A group of hotel rooms reserved (or "held") without deposit.

BOGO   Acronym for "buy one, get one free."

booked   Hotel rooms or other travel services, such as car rentals, that are reserved for a particular guest.

Problem Solving

Lower the Overhead

Minimizing overhead costs is important to the success of any business. These costs are essential to maintaining the day-to-day operation of any establishment, but if they rise above an acceptable level they can threaten your profits and, ultimately, the business itself. Business owners should remain vigilant for wasteful practices and should seek to implement key strategies to reduce overhead. And, of course, it is important to revisit these strategies on a regular basis and revise them to maximize operating efficiency.

booking Refers to a completed sale by any agency within the hospitality industry.

bounce back coupon Coupon given to the customer after a purchase is made, in the hopes that he or she has an incentive to redeem it within a certain period of time.

boutique hotel A small luxury hotel featuring premium services that is typically located in a fashionable district.

break-even point Minimum amount of sales that a restaurant must achieve in order to cover all costs.

brigade system The traditional kitchen organization system. Each position has a station and a set of well-defined responsibilities.

bubble dancer A tongue-in-cheek colloquialism for a dishwasher.

buried Overwhelmed. *See* **in the weeds**.

business travel Travel primarily motivated by business rather than personal interests.

bussing Clearing off and resetting tables after guests have left. In most restaurants, this is accomplished by the busboy (or "busser").

campers Restaurant guests who linger at their table long after their meal courses have been completed, sometimes obstructing further business by limiting seating capacity.

carrier Any provider of mass transportation, usually used in reference to an airline.

cash-in sheet A "cash-in" is used to account for all money collected during an employee's shift.

casual dining A restaurant providing sit-down service in a relaxed atmosphere. Menu prices are moderate and dress is informal.

central reservation system A system by which guests can make a reservation for a number of different hotels by contacting a single agency.

chaffing dish A metal dish that is filled with water and kept warm with a candle or fuel cell underneath. These are typically used on buffets.

chamber of commerce An association of local business people who specialize in local economic development, including tourism promotion.

charter group A party of travelers, usually touring together on a custom itinerary.

check cover   A book for transporting the check and payment between the server and the customer.

chef   The person who oversees the creation of a menu, recipes, ordering kitchen supplies and ingredients, and kitchen management.

chef de partie   The head of a section of a kitchen; for example, the vegetable section, pastry section, and so on.

commis   An apprentice cook who works under the tutelage of the chef de partie to learn the section and its responsibilities.

commissions   A percentage of the total product cost earned by selling the product to the customer.

comp   To give away for free. Items are typically "comped" by owners or managers for important customers or in an effort to attract future business or assuage complaints.

company culture   The atmosphere governing decisions made in a company concerning how problems and staff management are handled.

competitive analysis   Gathering information about competitors (for example, their services, prices, and vendors) in order to compete with them.

complimentary room   An occupied room for which the guest is not charged.

condominium hotels   Customers purchase equity in the hotel's guestrooms. Unit owners may live in the hotels permanently, use them as non-primary homes, or rent them independently or through the hotel's management company.

convention and visitors bureau   These organizations are local tourism marketing outfits that specialize in organizing conventions, meetings, conferences and visitations to a city, county, or region.

conversion study   Research studies used to analyze whether or not advertising respondents were convinced to become travelers as a result of advertising and follow-up material.

co-op advertising   Advertising funded by multiple destinations and/or suppliers.

cooperative marketing   Marketing programs that involve two or more participant companies, institutions, or organizations.

cooperative partner   An independent firm or organization that works with a tourism office by providing money or contributions in order to expand the marketing impact of the program of the tourism office.

core menu concept The overall type of menu on offer, based on a restaurant's cuisine and general concept.

corporation A type of ownership that is separate from individual owners. An advantage to becoming a corporation is personal, non-business asset protection in lawsuits.

corrective feedback The process of letting employees know what is expected and implementing correct procedures.

corrosion-resistant materials Surfaces that will retain their original qualities despite coming into contact with cleaning solutions, foods, or other materials.

cost of goods The total dollar amount (tallied daily, weekly, monthly, or annually) of all inventoried consumable items used in a restaurant.

cover A customer (for example, "It was a slow night—we only did 25 covers.").

credit card commissions A fee paid to credit card companies based upon a contracted percentage of credit card charges accepted.

credits Amount due from the vendor to a restaurant in restitution for a mispicked, damaged, or out of date product. *See* mispicked.

cremate it To burn something or prepare it until it is overcooked. *See* **kill it**.

cross contamination Cross contamination occurs when bacteria or chemicals from one product are allowed contact with another product. An example would be storing vegetables under a meat product in a way that allows meat drippings to contaminate the vegetables stored below.

cryovac Typically used with meat products, but many dried goods are also packed this way to maintain freshness. Cryovacing is a process that removes any excess oxygen from a bag, followed by the bag being heat-sealed to make it airtight. When receiving cryovaced meat products it is wise to check for discoloration, which indicates the airtight seal has been broken and the product should be immediately returned to the vendor.

curb sign A sign placed outside a business in order to display specials, menus, or artwork.

CTRLA Car and Truck Rental and Leasing Association.

CVB Convention and Visitors Bureau.

day-part Breaks items down by the culinary time of day, describing when menu items are served in a restaurant (such as the breakfast menu, lunch menu, and dinner menu).

demographic survey A survey taken in order to determine consumer habits based on age, gender, income, race, and so on. Used to help decide if a restaurant or menu item will be popular in a given area.

dessert A meal course that is typically sweet instead of savory, often served after the main entree is completed.

destination clubs The newest entry in lodging, this niche most closely resembles country clubs in terms of the framework of ownership. While developers of destination clubs hope to branch out into other price segments, for now this niche targets the most affluent of travelers. Customers pay initiation fees that can run as high as $500,000 and annual dues costing as much as $25,000. In return, customers get to stay for weeks at a time in multi-million dollar residences and villas in prime urban and resort locations and enjoy a full range of amenities and services.

deuce A table with only two seating places.

destination A hotel, resort, attraction, city, or any other target of travel.

destination marketing Marketing a city, state, country, area, or region to travelers and trade.

destination marketing organization Local tourism marketing groups (for example, convention and visitors bureaus or chambers of commerce).

discounted fare Less expensive air fare negotiated for convention, trade show, meeting, group, and corporate travelers.

"Discover America" Motto used by the Travel Industry Association and its marketing partners to market travel within the United States.

double Two shifts worked in a row.

double/triple sat When more than one table is seated in a particular station at a specific time.

dramshop laws Laws regarding establishments that serve alcoholic beverages to the public.

drink cost Daily, weekly, monthly, or annual total cost in dollars of all items regarding the cost of drink sales inventoried in a restaurant.

drop To begin cooking the accompanying item (as in, "The mussels are almost done, drop the calamari now.").

drop the check To deliver a guest's bill to their table for payment.

drop food/order The act of beginning to prepare a customer's food; the act of a waiter delivering an order to the customers.

dual-branding When multiple brand name organizations are located in the same retail space.

dupe The ticket that gets submitted to the kitchen telling the cooks what orders to prepare.

duxelle A finely chopped blend of mushrooms that can be used in stuffings, soups, and cold spreads.

dying/dead Food that is unservable because of incorrect temperature, appearance, or ingredients. (For example, "My steak's dying in the pass because I do not have vegetables to go with it!")

early bird Generally an elderly person or tourist who wants everything included for very little cost. (An example is a $9.99 "all-you-can-eat" buffet.)

early bird special An inexpensive meal that is typically available for a limited amount of time, often just when the restaurant opens for service.

egress Regarding how easy it is for a restaurant's customers to exit the parking lot.

eighty-six (86) A colloquial expression, either meaning that an item has run out or that an item should be gotten rid of due to ingredient expiration or menu changes. Sometimes jokingly used to refer to termination of employment.

entrée The term normally refers to the main course of a meal, but can also mean any major course.

expediter The kitchen staff who groups plated food together, by table number, for the servers to deliver. The expediter is in charge of putting together the components and the proper presentation of dishes before they are delivered to the tables by the server or food-runner.

facilities Core physical features, for example accommodations, restaurants, bars, and conference rooms.

fam tours Organized trips for travel agents, tour operators, tour wholesalers, or other members of the travel industry for the purpose of educating and "familiarizing" them with specific destinations. By seeing the destinations where they are sending travelers, the travel trade is better prepared to answer customer queries and promote travel to that destination.

feasibility study A study performed to see if a concept might work.

feeder airport/city An outlying location that feeds travelers to hubs or gateway cities.

FIFO (first in, first out)   Rotating and using products according to date of expiration or when they were received.

fire it!   Jargon used to let a cook know when to begin cooking a particular item, usually given to be timed with an entire order.

FIT (free independent travel)   Individual travel in which an operator has arranged blocks of rooms at separate destinations for use by individual travelers. These travelers move independently, not in a group, often by rental car or public transportation.

fixed costs   The continuous permanent costs that do not vary (such as rent, leases, and loans).

food contact surfaces   Any surfaces that come in contact with food.

food cost   What a menu item or dish costs to prepare. The cost of an entrée is tallied by adding the cost of meat, sauce, vegetables, and starch, for example. Most restaurants run a 30 to 40 percent food cost, though this does not include the cost of overhead that needs to be added in before a restaurant starts making a profit.

foodie   The bane of cooks and chefs everywhere; a nonprofessional cook/chef with pretensions to connoisseurship. Typically snobbish and self-trained, or trained only in various culinary classes for nonprofessionals.

food runner   A serving assistant whose principal duty is to deliver food to tables once order assembly is finished by the expediter. The food runner may also assist in drink-filling, bussing, or expediting if others are busy.

franchise   The right to market a service and/or product often exclusively for a specified area, as granted by the manufacturer, developer, or distributor in return for a fee. Franchises are common in the fast food industry, but increasingly adopted within the hotel community.

franchisee   Owner of a franchise.

franchising   The decision to market a business, or services or goods, for a fee or a percentage of the gross sales. Restaurants can design a franchise agreement allowing others to use their name, advertising, expertise, and concept for a fee.

frequency   The number of times an advertisement comes up during a given campaign.

frequent independent traveler (FIT)   Designation that applies to visitors who arrive on their own as opposed to being a part of an organized party.

front office An office normally located in the lobby whose main function is to coordinate the sale of guest rooms, provide keys and mail, maintain guest accounts, print bills, collect payments, and provide information to other areas within the hotel.

front of house Refers to the area of a restaurant where guests are allowed; for example, the dining room and bar are front of the house.

fulfillment Servicing customers and trade personnel who request information as a result of advertising or promotional programs. Services often include an 800 number, sales staff, and distribution of materials.

full service A full service restaurant is one where a staff member is available to see to the customer's every need.

garde-manger Pantry chef. The position responsible for cold food preparation, including salads, cold appetizers, and dessert-plating.

gateway or gateway city A transportation hub through which tourists and travelers enter the area from outside the region.

GIT (groups independent travel) Group travel in which individuals buy a group package allowing them to travel with others using a pre-established itinerary.

goodwill The value of a business or a business's assets or the positive reputation/rapport a business has earned with its customers.

group rate Lower negotiated hotel rate for convention, trade show, meeting, tour, or incentive group.

guest account An itemized record of a guest's charges and credits, maintained by the front office and presented at the time of the guest's departure. Also referred to as a guest bill, guest folio, or guest statement.

guest amenities Not to be confused with "amenities," this is the term given to the range of consumable items provided in guest room bathrooms, often including such items as shampoo, lotion, conditioner, soap, toothpaste, toothbrush, shower caps, and so on. The cost of these items are included in room rate.

guest check The bill presented to restaurant and bar patrons for food and beverage consumed during a visit. Also referred to as a waiter's check or restaurant check.

guest history A record maintained for each guest who has stayed at the hotel with a separate entry for each visit and details of relevant preferences. This is a useful reference tool for reservations, marketing, and credit departments. Guest histories are now more readily available due to the increased use of computers and technology.

guest house   A personal residence with limited overnight accommodation sometimes constrained by legislation and residence concerns. Typically provides breakfast, which is included in the room rate, but no other meals. Guest houses are not commercially licensed to provide alcoholic beverages.

guest service directory   A documented list of all of the features of a hotel together with general and germane information about the community within which the hotel is located. Directories are typically provided within each guest room.

HACCP (Hazard Analysis Control Point System)   Helps ensure food-handling errors do not occur and that safe food is served to customers.

head in beds   Industry jargon referring to the main marketing objective of accommodations and most destinations (that is, to increase the number of overnight stays).

high (peak) season/shoulder season   The period of consecutive months during which hospitality businesses enjoy the greatest profit.

hockey puck   A well-done hamburger.

hold time   The time you are allowed to hold an item before it begins to break down.

hospitality industry   Alternate name for the travel industry.

host/hostess   The person who greets the guests and shows them to their table. The host is also responsible for keeping track of reservations and waiting lines.

hotel   A facility providing room (and often board) to travelers. A hotel may provide food and beverage services on site (but not always within the accommodation building), usually by in-house staff (but occasionally through an outside food and beverage contractor). A hotel may or may not provide a range of recreation and other amenities on site or by arrangement with others off site. This group includes motels, resort hotels or resorts, and commercial hotels.

hotel representative   An individual or firm responsible for facilitating market accessibility to a hotel property by the travel trade.

HQSC   Hospitality, quality, service, and cleanliness.

hub   An airport or city that serves as a central connecting point for aircraft, trains, or buses from outlying feeder airports or cities.

hub and spoke   Air carriers utilization of selected cities as "hubs" for connections to regional destinations.

HVAC   Heating, ventilation, and air conditioning.

icon   A landmark that is typically associated with a destination.

image advertising   Determining the good qualities of your product or service, and advertising these good qualities.

incentive travel   Travel offered as a reward for top performance, or the industry that creates, markets, and coordinates these programs.

inclusive tour   A tour program that includes a variety of features for a single rate, such as airfare, accommodations, guided tours, shows, and so on.

ingress and egress   refers to the means of entering and leaving an establishment.

innkeepers statutes   Statutes that limit the common law liability of innkeepers.

intelligent hotels   Hotels featuring state-of-the-art technology systems. These hotels have replaced the antiquated systems to reduce energy costs and typically have integrated systems that couple the analog and digital systems to achieve an effective communication within their establishment.

international marketing   Marketing a destination, product, or service to customers and the trade outside of the United States.

in the weeds   Can have meanings for both the front and back of the house of a restaurant. A kitchen in the weeds might have only one two-foot by three-foot grill and a 40-person order for medium-well steaks in the space of five minutes. In the front of the house, it could mean one server just had two parties of 15 seated at the same time and everyone wants separate checks.

jeopardy/wheel of fortune crowd   Early bird diners who want to eat and return home early, usually on the lookout for inexpensive meals that include everything for one price.

kill it   To burn something badly or overcook it. *See* **cremate it**.

kitchenware   multi-use utensils other than tableware.

leisure travel   Travel for recreational, educational, sightseeing, relaxing, or other experiential purposes.

limited liability company (LLC)   A legal form of business company in the United States offering limited liability to its owners.

limited service hotels   Brand hotels without a restaurant.

line   The line is the area that divides the cooks from the wait staff. It is where the food is placed to await pickup.

line cook   A cook who works under the direction of the chef or kitchen manager. Usually in charge of a specific facet of cooking or dish preparation.

loss of attraction   "Loss of attraction" falls under the Business Income and Extra Expense insurance coverage form, although coverage is rarely included as it is hard to prove. For example, if a fire occurred at a hotel in Las Vegas, there could be other hotels in the surrounding area with lost income as a result of the reduction in tourism. For those hotels that have not suffered direct damage to the property, business income claims would fall under "loss of attraction." Loss of attraction coverage is uncommon and it can be difficult to assess the loss resulting from a disaster and differentiate it from that which could have resulted from poor management or other uninsured factors.

low (off-peak) season   The months during which the lowest revenues are generated.

LTO (limited time offer)   Used in advertising to let the customer know that the special sale, offer, or product price does not reflect a permanent state of affairs and should be taken advantage of while on offer.

margin markup   The difference between the price a manufacturer charges a distributor and the amount the distributor, in turn, charges the customer. A margin markup sometimes allows a customer to negotiate with a distributor.

market penetration   Growing a business to gain more of the market share.

market saturation   A term used to describe a situation in which a product is diffused (distributed) within a market.

market share   The percentage of business within a market category.

market volume   The total number of travelers within a market category.

meat jobber   A distributor or wholesaler that sells to restaurants.

menu   A catalogue of dishes and beverages available in a restaurant.

mini bar   A small and specially-designed, floor-mounted refrigerator containing a variety of beverages and snack. Mini bars are often found in guest rooms, with individual guest room key access. This amenity is often a more profitable substitute for room service.

mise en place   Refers to the set up of the sauté station. Essentially, it means everything in its place. Most cooks put certain ingredients they intend to use in specific spots for their shifts, and different cooks have different versions of mise en place.

mispick   An item that is ordered from a vendor that has a label on it that does not match the product it contains.

mission (sales)   A promotional and sales trip coordinated by state travel offices, convention and visitors bureaus, or key industry member whose purpose is to increase product awareness, boost sales, and to enhance overall image.

M.O.D.   Manager on duty.

motel   Overnight accommodation originally targeted to automobile travelers and, therefore, situated at roadside locations. Originally coined by combining the words *motor* and *hotel*, a motel offers accommodation only, with no other amenities or services provided.

motorcoach   Deluxe bus used by most tour operators for group tour programs. Amenities include, but are not limited to, reclining seats, full bathrooms, air conditioning, overhead lighting, and refreshments.

mystery shopper   Someone who is asked to visit a restaurant and evaluate its performance.

net rate   The rate provided to wholesalers and tour operators that can be marked up before sale to a customer.

net sales   This is the actual dollar amount of all items sold, excluding sales tax.

no call   Employee who fails to appear to work and does not call; a reservation that does not show up and does not call.

no show   A customer with a reservation at a restaurant or hotel who fails to show up and does not cancel.

NTA   National Tour Association, composed of domestic tour operators.

nuke it   To microwave something.

occupancy (occ percentage/occ rate)   The percentage of available rooms occupied for a period of time, it is calculated by dividing the number of rooms occupied by the number of rooms available for the same period.

on a rail or on the fly   Something needed quickly (as in "I need a side of fries on the fly").

on-the-fly   A directive given to a line cook when a food item is needed in a hurry. Usually employed when an item is returned to be re-cooked or when a server forgets to place an order on time. (The term *rush-it* may also be applied in these instances.)

on-the-rocks   A cocktail or beverage over cubes of ice.

open door policy   The policy in a restaurant that lets employees know management is always available to talk about any concerns.

outsourcing   Paying for a job done by someone who is not under employment of the organization.

overbooking   A circumstance in which a hotel has taken more room reservations than it is able to accommodate. Hotels that utilize overbooking as a means for ensuring full capacity are increasingly being monitored by tour wholesalers and operators in an attempt to better minimize the collateral damage such policies often create.

overhead   The factors added up when costing out menu products to make sure a profit is being made. Overhead may include electricity costs, paper and chemical products, employee salaries and any additional costs pertinent in serving any item.

package   Term used to describe an assembly of individual components under a single-price system. Typically, the package price includes return transportation, ground transfers, baggage handling, accommodation, meals, and taxes. Car rentals, recreation, and some entertainment may also be included but are usually supplementary to the core package price.

paddy well   A term used very frequently in Irish pubs and restaurants, meaning to cook something until there is no possibility of life remaining. (The next level above being "cremate it.")

paid outs   Money taken from the register to purchase items with cash for the restaurant. A record is always kept of each transaction along with a receipt.

partnership   When two or more people go into business together and share all liability, assets, and profits.

party   A self-contained group of two or more who have gathered to dine at an eating establishment.

pass station The area of a restaurant where food is passed from the kitchen to wait staff.

peaks and valleys The highs and lows of the travel season. Travel industry marketers are challenged to implement programs to build consistent year-round business and offset the "peaks and valleys."

perceived value In a customer's estimation, the value attached to a product or service.

pittsburgh rare Burnt on the outside, rare on the inside.

plating The act of putting food on a plate. This includes adding any sauce or garnish before passing the plate over to an expeditor or server.

point of distinction The place where a particular restaurant differs from all others.

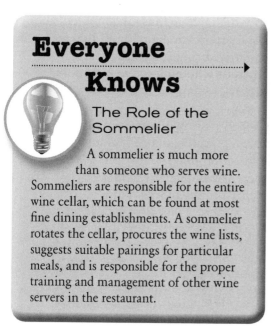

Everyone Knows

The Role of the Sommelier

A sommelier is much more than someone who serves wine. Sommeliers are responsible for the entire wine cellar, which can be found at most fine dining establishments. A sommelier rotates the cellar, procures the wine lists, suggests suitable pairings for particular meals, and is responsible for the proper training and management of other wine servers in the restaurant.

point of purchase Generally the place where customers pay for their items.

POS system A point-of-sale computer system helps businesses track their sales. It can also track individual employee sales and monitor the frequency with which dishes are sold.

pow wow The largest international travel marketplace held in the United States, sponsored by the Travel Industry Association of America.

press release The primary tool used to tell the story of a business. It is a brief, concise snippet that is submitted to the media for possible publication. It should include the five W's—who, what, where, when, and why.

press trips Organized trips for travel writers and broadcasters to help in the preparation of stories about tourism destinations. Journalists usually travel independently with the assistance of a state's office of tourism.

prime interest rate   The interest rate that banks reserve for their most credit-worthy customers.

productivity   A measure of scheduling efficiency.

property   A hotel, motel, inn, lodge, or other accommodation facility.

pump it out   Getting food quickly out of the kitchen and to customers.

push it   Jargon for "sell it." (For example, "Push the lamb tonight, we need to use it before it expires.")

quick services restaurant (QSR)   A fast food restaurant.

rack rate   The rate accommodations publically quoted. Group rates, convention, trade show, meeting, and incentive travel rates are negotiated separately by hotels and program organizers.

ratatouille   A vegetable stew originating in Provence, France, made with tomatoes, peppers, eggplant, onions, garlic, and zucchini (all of which are stewed). Can be served hot or cold.

reach   The percentage of people within a specific target audience reached by an advertising campaign.

reach-in   A refrigeration unit or freezer unit small enough that a person can reach in to access the unit's contents but not big enough to be entered. Units housed below production surfaces or on the floor in production areas are often referred to as "lowboys."

receptive operator   Specializes in coordinating arrangements for incoming visitors at a destination, including airport transfers, sightseeing, restaurants and nightclubs, accommodations, and so on.

redneck   The non-tipping public—not referring to a rural type person, but rather meaning a cheapskate *See* **stiffs**.

refer   A slang term for a refrigeration unit.

registration card (reg. card)   The form on which arriving guests write their names, addresses, and other requested information such mode of transportation used, nationality, purpose of visit (usually business or pleasure), method of payment, and length of stay. A space is also provided for signature, room rate, and room number.

repeat business   Business that returns continually, thereby generating increased profits.

reprimand   A documented notice or action that is given to an employee who disregards restaurant policies and kept in the employee's file.

reservation systems (automation vendors)   Computerized systems leased to travel agencies offering airline, hotel, car rental, and selected tour availability and bookings.

resort hotels and spas   Properties that cater primarily to vacationers and tourists that typically offer more recreational amenities and services, in a more aesthetically pleasing setting, than other hotels. These hotels are located in attractive and natural tourism destinations and their clientele are groups and couples seeking adventure combined with sophistication and comfort. The attractions vary depending on the region, with some offering golf, tennis, scuba diving, and, depending on the natural surroundings, other recreational activities.

retail agent   A travel agent.

retailer   Another term for travel agents who sell travel products directly to customers.

revenue per available room (RevPAR)   Revenue per available room, RevPAR is the primary performance indicator for hotels and consists of an equation: RevPAR = occupancy (percentage of available rooms occupied) x average room rate per night. RevPAR can be used to compare companies, but only if they have broadly similar hotels (that is, if they are similarly priced and in similar locations). Most hotel companies give regional breakdowns of RevPAR, which can be compared with the RevPAR of other hotels.

rollup   Silverware rolled into a linen or paper napkin.

room   Unit occupied by customer at a hotel property. Types of rooms include: double (no guarantee of two beds), double double (two double beds or two queens or kings), and twin (two twin beds or two doubles or queens).

room block   A pre-established number of rooms reserved in advance for group use (for a conference or tour, for example).

room service   Food and drink delivered and served in a guest room.

sacked   Fired, usually after a major screw-up (such as serving a banquet of 200 people the $100 bottles of Dom Perignon champagne instead of the $12.95 bottles intended for service).

safe materials   Materials that will not have a negative impact on a food product.

safety deposit boxes   Individual boxes provided for safekeeping guest valuables. Located either in a secure and supervised location or within the guest rooms themselves.

sales mission   Where suppliers from one DMO travel together to a prearranged place collectively promote travel to their area. These missions often include educational seminars for travel agents and tour operators.

sales seminar   An educational session in which travel industry members assemble to learn about tourism destinations.

sanitizing   A cleaning process used to remove anything unhygienic.

saucier or sauté chef   The chef de partie responsible for all sautéed items and their sauces.

sections   Many restaurant dining rooms are divided into sections, and each section goes to a particular wait staff during each shift.

server   The representative of the eating establishment who takes orders, serves food and drinks, and tends to the needs of dining guests.

server's assistant   The position is also sometimes known as bus person, busser, assistant waiter or food runner. This person, along with the server, helps tend to the needs of a table of customers. The server assistant's duties may include filling beverage glasses, delivering food, removing unwanted dishes, or taking small orders. The server's assistant is sometimes also "server-in-training."

sharking   The process of luring an employee from one restaurant to another.

shelf life   The amount of time in storage that a product can maintain quality, freshness, and edibility.

shorting   An unscrupulous method used by some vendors to charge a restaurant for more of a particular product than the restaurant actually receives.

shoulder season   The period between peak and low season.

side-work   The "odd jobs" assigned to service staff such as stocking, cleaning, and rolling silverware.

single service articles   Disposable tableware in the form of carry-out utensils designed for one-time or single customer use.

site inspection   Assessment of a destination or facility by a conference planner, convention or trade show manager, site selection committee, tour operator, wholesaler, or incentive travel manager to determine the satisfaction of specific needs prior to deciding on an appropriate place for an event. Sometimes, following site selection, an inspection may be utilized to make arrangements.

sizzle platter Heavy-grade, metal, oval plate that is used to reheat or cook something in a high-temperature oven.

skate Leave without doing sidework.

slammed Busy. (Slightly less disastrous than "in the weeds.")

sole proprietorship A business that is owned and operated by one person.

sommelier Wine steward or wine waiter.

sous chef The sous chef serves directly under the executive chef as second-in-command of the kitchen.

spouse program Special activities planned for peripheral attendees of conventions, trade shows, or meetings.

stair-stepping Scheduling employees at different, staggered intervals with the intention of improving productivity.

starch Starch can mean potatoes, rice, grain, or pasta and typically accompanies the vegetable with a plated meal.

star rating system A *five-star hotel* is the most expensive hotel/resort with numerous amenities designed to enhance the quality of the client's stay; a *four-star hotel* is a first class establishment that is expensive (by middle-class standards), with many "luxury" services; a *three-star hotel* is a moderately priced hotel with maid service, room service, Internet access, and a swimming pool; a *two-star hotel* is a reasonably priced hotel that usually features daily maid service; a *one-star hotel* is an inexpensive hotel, often without maid or room service; and *no category hotels* include motels, cottages, bungalows, and other lodging facilities with limited services.

station The set number of tables waited on by a particular server.

stiffed Colloquial term used to describe a situation where a customer does not leave a gratuity for service, although a gratuity was expected.

still moving or still mooing Ultra rare (as in, "They want the tender still mooing").

streetfighting Marketing your store in your immediate neighborhood by distributing flyers on car windshields, donating food to businesses, working with community-based organizations, and so on.

stretch it To make limited orders of an item last through an entire shift by "stretching it" with whatever is available and edible.

supplier Business that provides industry products.

table turn   Number of times a table has had the full revolution of service from being seated to getting the check and then reset for the next group of customers.

tare   The weight of a container in which the product is shipped from a vendor. This weight must legally be deducted from the actual weight of the product.

target audience/market   A specific demographic, the target group at which marketing communications are directed.

target market analysis   Determining who the customers of a business are and designing marketing aimed at their profile.

target operating points   TRPOs are a statistical measurement that allows evaluation of the relative impact of differing ad campaigns.

tender   A tenderloin.

the man, the boogie man   A health inspector.

TIA   Travel Industry Association of America.

timeshare   Shared ownership of vacation real estate where purchasers acquire a period of time in a condominium, townhouse, apartment, or other type of accommodation.

tips   Money paid by customers directly to bartenders, servers, or other personnel for the services they have given. The amount given typically reflects the quality of service rendered.

top   The number of people in a dining party. For example, an "eight top" is a dining party of eight, while a "three top" is a party of three.

toss   An unscrupulous method used by some vendors to make a box look like it is full of product.

TOT   Transient Occupancy Tax.

totes   Plastic containers typically used to deliver fish. Totes are prized by kitchen staff because, once washed and sanitized, they make excellent airtight storage containers.

tourism   Leisure travel.

tourist/visitor/traveler   Any person who travels either for leisure or business purposes more than 100 miles (round-trip) in a day or who stays overnight away from his or her primary place of residence.

tourne   A vegetable that is cut to resemble a small, slightly-tapered cork—but instead of being smooth, it is cut to have seven equally large facets. Tournes are generally fashioned out of root vegetables, potatoes, carrots, but sometimes zucchini or other soft vegetables are used. Traditionally, tournes are boiled, steamed or roasted.

tour operator   A person who operates group travel, providing a complete experience for one price inclusive of transportation, accommodations, selected meals and, if necessary, a guide.

tour wholesaler   An individual or company that sells tour packages and tour product to travel agents.

trade area   The area surrounding a business, which provides its major customer base.

trade shows   Trade shows differ from conventions in that they feature exhibit areas that showcase product exhibition and sales opportunities for suppliers as well as information gathering and buying opportunities for customers.

traditional lodging   Accommodations in which guests pay nightly rates for single rooms or suites and have full access to the establishment's amenities and services. Rates vary based on time of week, season, and nearby events and attractions.

traffic counts   Surveys of actual foot traffic or motor traffic passing a restaurant.

transfer   The transportation of visitors between their point of arrival and selected hotel, and back again on departure day.

transient occupancy tax (TOT)   Also known as a bed tax, this is a local tax on the cost of commercial accommodations providers.

travel   Leisure and other travel including travel for business, medical care, or education. All tourism is travel, but not all travel is tourism.

travel agent   An individual who arranges travel for other individuals or groups. Travel agents often specialize, coordinating cruises, adventure travel, conventions, and meetings. Travel agents typically receive a 10 to 15 percent commission on whatever they coordinate.

travel trade   The collective term for tour operators, wholesalers, and travel agents.

triple-net lease   A lease requiring the individual who is leasing to pay all expenses (utilities, taxes, insurance, maintenance, and so on) in addition to rent.

turn and burn   Turn a table over quickly (usually because there is a long waiting list for tables).

turnover rate   The pace at which tables empty and re-fill during a shift. A high turnover rate means more people have eaten and

Professional
Ethics

Breaking the "Two Second Rule"

The "two second rule" rule was actually put to the test by Jillian Clarke at the University of Illinois in 2003. Ms. Clarke performed an experiment by contaminating ceramic tiles with *E. coli*, placing gummy bears and cookies on the tiles for the statutory two seconds, and then analyzing the foods. She found that they had, in fact, become contaminated with bacteria. Based on these findings, a general regard for customers' health, and basic common sense, an ethical waiter or chef would never employ the "two second rule" in the workplace. It is never worth risking the health of your customers and, by extension, your business.

left, while a comparatively slower turnover rate means the same people have been lingering at the table or the table is sitting empty.

two second rule   A rule that deems it safe to retrieve a piece of food from the floor and return it to its sauté pan or plate, provided little time (such as a few seconds) has elapsed.

upsell   To suggest a higher priced item. (Suggesting Iron Horse at $6.00 a glass as opposed to a house wine at $4.00 a glass is an example of upselling.)

utensil   Tableware and kitchenware that is used to cook or eat food.

variable costs   The costs in a business that do not remain the same, such as the cost of goods.

veg   The vegetable accompaniment to a plated meal.

VIP   A very important customer, perhaps well known and deserving of extra special treatment. Food critics fall into this category. A VIP is typically offered comps.

visitors center   Travel information center whose purpose is to help visitors plan their stays. A visitor center is typically operated by a convention and visitors bureau, chamber of commerce, or tourism organization.

vouchers   Forms or coupons provided to a traveler who purchases a tour proving that certain tour components have been prepaid.

Vouchers can be exchanged for tour components, such as accommodations, meals, sightseeing, theater tickets, and more during an actual trip.

waitron   Another title for a waiter or waitress, designed to be gender-neutral.

wake up call   A call made by the front office, usually by telephone, to a guest room at the established time a guest wishes to be awakened.

walked   Refers to a customer who left without paying the bill or an employee who quit and left during the middle of his or her shift.

walked guests   When a hotel is overbooked and a guest room is not available for a confirmed guest, the hotel may "walk" to a nearby hotel. Typically this includes paying for transportation to the hotel and covering any difference in price at the hotel to which the guest moved.

walk-in   A refrigeration unit or freezer unit large enough for a person to physically enter through its door, in contrast to the "reach-in," which is smaller and only allows for retrieval from the outside.

walk-in guest   Guest who checks in without a prior reservation.

waste factor   A consideration made when adding a percentage to food costs in order to account for food waste or loss.

well drinks   "Well" drinks are made with inexpensive house liquors. For example, if a customer asks for a gin and tonic without specifying a particular brand of gin, he or she will get whatever moderately priced gin the house has on hand.

wholesaler   Sales representatives who develop and market inclusive tours and individual travel programs to the consumer through travel agents. Wholesalers do not sell directly to the public.

window   A shelf, often heated, upon which the food is placed in preparation for delivery to a table.

working for tips   Colloquial term used to describe persons whose main income is dependent on the gratuities they earn and not on the wages they are paid.

yield   The total amount of usable product remaining after unusable parts are excised.

Chapter 6

Resources

If you have read through this guide, you have a strong working knowledge of the hospitality industry. But, as with anything else, there is always more to learn. Accordingly, this chapter outlines additional sources where you can turn to gather further information and gain an even greater perspective. These sources include associations and organizations—including schools—books and periodicals, and Web sites.

Associations and Organizations

In many industries, joining a professional association or organization is essential (and sometimes even required). Membership in such a group can be beneficial in many ways. For starters, it is certainly useful for networking purposes. The old adage that "it's not what you know, it's who you know" remains true (if somewhat hyperbolic). The following associations and organizations provide invaluable contacts and information for industry insiders and newcomers alike.

The American Culinary Federation, Inc. (ACF) is a professional organization for chefs and cooks, dedicated to promoting a positive public image of the profession. The organization offers competitions, certification programs, regional and national conferences, and programs to connect masters with willing apprentices. (http://www.restaurant.org)

American Gaming Association (AGA) was founded in June 1995 in Washington, D.C. The goal of the organization is to create a better understanding of the gaming entertainment industry by bringing facts about the industry to the gambling public, politicians, and other officials. Another one of its major goals is to advocate for the industry. This Web site provides information on current trends in the industry as well as available jobs. The American Gaming Association also assists the commercial casino industry by addressing federal regulatory laws that affect its members. (http://www.americangaming.com)

The Brewers Association is, according to its mission statement, "an organization of brewers, for brewers and by brewers." It comprises more than 1,000 U.S. brewery members. The association is made up of trade members as well as beer wholesalers, all dedicated to the promotion of small-batch brewing. (http://www.beertown.org)

Fast Facts

Feeding the Country

On any given day in the United States, 130 million people will be served food at some kind of eating establishment.

National Restaurant Association is a member of the International Hotel & Restaurant Association (IH&RA). It claims itself "a network of national associations, international chains, hotel operators, restaurateurs and supplier companies in more than 150 countries, representing over 750,000 establishments." The association works to develop and promote industry standards, watch out for industry trends, and share information and best practices with restaurateurs nationwide. (http://www.restaurant.org)

SlowFood is a non-profit, "eco-gastronomic" member-supported organization. It was founded in 1989 with the intention of challenging the fast food world. This group remains nostalgic for lost local food traditions. It also aims to better inform people in their food choices and how they affect the world around them. To do that, the Slow Food philosophy marries the concepts of pleasure and responsibility, deeming them "inseparable." This is a useful site for people interested in sustainable food production. (http://slowfood.com)

USDA Foreign Agricultural Service maintains Export.gov, a resource-rich Web site where interested parties can learn about international sales as well as how to "avoid pitfalls such as non-payment and intellectual property misappropriation." The purpose of this site is improved customer service for businesses working with the Federal Government. The USDA brings together resources from across the U.S. government to assist American businesses in planning their international sales strategies and succeed in the global marketplace. From market research and trade leads from the U.S. Department of Commerce's Commercial Service to export finance information from Export-Import Bank and the Small Business Administration to agricultural export assistance from USDA, Export.gov helps American exporters navigate the international sales process and avoid pitfalls such as non-payment and intellectual property misappropriation. Export.gov was created to provide better customer service for businesses interacting with the federal government. It is managed by the U.S. Department of Commerce's International Trade Administration. (http://www.export.gov)

Educational Institutions

ABC Bartending Schools can be found all over the United States. Their Web site provides a list of the cities where ABC programs are offered. These schools also offer job placement around the country, regardless of the location attended. In addition to the standard courses offered at any school, ABC classes instruct in techniques related to speed, mixology, keg-tapping, customer service, résumés and interviews, alcohol awareness, and flair training. (http://www.abcbartending.com)

California Culinary Academy is nestled within California's famous wine country. It now partners with the famous Le Cordon Bleu culinary school, marrying the hospitality-training program with a top-notch culinary program. The California Culinary Academy offers a certificate program in baking and pastry arts, as well as an associate's degree program in culinary arts, hospitality, and restaurant management. (http://www.cookingschool-california.com)

Cornell University School of Hotel Administration is considered one of the most prestigious such programs in the world. It offers a bachelor of science in hotel administration, a master's degree in hospitality management, and a master's of science and Ph.D. in hotel administration. Cornell University is located near

Cayuga Lake in Ithaca, New York. It was founded by Ellsworth Statler (a wealthy hotel magnate). The Statler Hotel allows students to gain hands-on experiences before they graduate. Cornell has a high job placement rate: 75 percent of undergraduates receive job offers, while 20 percent continue their education. Starting salaries for undergraduates reach as high as $60,000. Seventy-seven percent of graduates with master's degrees are placed in jobs, with starting salaries ranging from $63,000 to $90,000. (http://www.hotelschool.cornell.edu)

Court of Master Sommeliers was established to encourage better standards of beverage knowledge and service in hotels and restaurants. Education is the Court's foremost responsibility. There are four stages necessary in attaining the top qualifications of master sommelier: introductory sommelier course, certified sommelier exam, advanced sommelier exam, and master sommelier diploma exam. The letters "MS" after a candidate's name tell an employer that a sommelier is a professional beverage manager and can control an efficient, profitable beverage service. Over the two decades since the Court's first examination was held, 171 candidates have earned master sommelier diplomas. In the service of wine, spirits, and other alcoholic beverages, the master sommelier diploma is the ultimate professional credential attainable worldwide. Individuals who successfully complete all parts of the master sommelier diploma are expected to uphold the accepted ethics and standards of the Court of Master Sommeliers. Recipients of the diploma are required to sign an agreement binding them to the code of ethics and conduct of master sommeliers. (http://mastersommeliers.org)

The Culinary Institute of America is one of the largest and most prestigious cooking schools in the United States, with campuses in Hyde Park and St. Helena in New York as well as in California's Napa Valley. The Institute offers a strong academic program, six professional baking and cooking suites in each of its locations, and a full restaurant where interns can hone their skills at the Napa Valley Greystone campus. Students at this institute can obtain professional wine certification. Graduates can complete programs awarding them pro-chef certification. Graduates often continue on to work in some of the best restaurants across the country. *Food and Wine* magazine listed five of CIA's graduates in its 2009 issue on the Top 10 Best New Chefs in America. (http://www.ciachef.edu)

The French Culinary Institute of New York City is a school renowned worldwide for its excellent training. The culinary institution is dedicated to training its students to be the absolute best in the industry. The French Culinary Institute insists that its students totally immerse themselves in their passion for cooking. It recently introduced a new brand of Italian cooking that allows the student chef to immerse him- or herself in the language, history, and culture of Italian cooking in order to better understand the preparation of its food. (http://www.frenchculinary.com)

Gateway Gourmet.com is focused on those individuals interested in a culinary career that do not live on either the East or West coast of the United States. This Web site provides information on the top culinary and hospitality schools all over the country. While it suggests recipes, its main purpose is to give a comprehensive list of cooking school guides, careers, and helpful information on finding the right career within the field. (http://www.gatewaygourmet.com)

Nick Kallos Casino Gaming School is located in Las Vegas. Its mission is to help casino dealers be the best in the business. Students take classes for five hours a day, four days a week. The school has flexible hours and will work with students at their own paces. Courses include blackjack, craps, roulette, poker, pai gow poker, and mini baccarat. Each course is 80 hours long. After attending Kallos' schools, graduates are guaranteed lifetime placement assistance and job practice. Dealing techniques taught at this school can be used in all of the major casinos around the country. (http://www.learntodeal.com)

Book and Periodicals

Books

Introduction to Management in the Hospitality Industry, **Seventh Edition.** By Clayton W. Barrows and Tom Powers (John Wiley and Sons, 2002). This book offers a comprehensive treatment of the entire hospitality industry, thoroughly updated to reflect the latest trends in the hospitality, foodservice, and travel/tourism industries. It provides learning objectives, summaries, review questions, and key terms and concepts, along with real-life case histories.

Historic Hotels of the World, Past and Present. By Robert B. Ludy (David McKay Company, 1927). This book offers a detailed overview of the hotel industry from its inception in biblical times through the 1920's. This tome discusses the history of various hotels in a Victorian tone, which is at times challenging to the modern sensibility.

The Hotel and Restaurant Business, **Sixth Edition.** By Donald E. Lundberg (John Wiley and Sons, 1994). This book offers an excellent introduction to the industry as well as a wealth of practical, how-to information for anyone entering the field. Based on the author's more than 30 years of experience in hospitality. *The Hotel and Restaurant Business* offers comprehensive information on the background and current status of the industry, presented in an interesting, easy-to-read style. New chapters provide up-to-date information on hospitality-specific human resources and human relations issues, the global nature of the hotel and restaurant business, recent changes in hotel development and financing brought about by the 2008–2009 recession, growth in the institutional segment of the restaurant business, and changes in the fast-food business and fast-food franchising.

Kitchen Confidential: Adventures in the Culinary Underbelly. By Anthony Bourdain (Harper Perrenial, 2001). This book, released in 2000, is both Bourdain's professional memoir and a behind-the-scenes look at restaurant kitchens. He describes in graphic detail the ins and outs of the restaurant trade. The book is remarkable for its insistence in deglamorizing the professional culinary industry. The commercial kitchen is described as an intense, unpleasant and sometimes hazardous place of work staffed by what he describes as "misfits." Bourdain is absolutely insistent that this is no place for hobbyists. Anyone entering this industry will run away screaming, he insists, if they lack an almost masochistic, perhaps irrational, dedication to cooking.

Best Practice

Be Professional

Everyone in bartending school learns how to mix drinks. So how can you set yourself apart from the rest (and get a recommendation for employment from your instructors)? Be professional. Distinguish yourself from the crowd by arriving early, following directions, minding your appearance, and always maintaining a positive attitude.

Periodicals

All About Beer provides information for the beer lover. It covers beer tastings, reviews, and current industry trends. (http://www.allaboutbeer.com)

Bon Appetit features stories on food, entertainment, and wine. (http://www.bonappetit.com)

Casino Journal covers the casino industry in North America. Articles also feature new technologies, competition within the industry, and casino management. (http://www.casinojournal.com)

Decanter features vintages, wine industry trends, and recommendations. (http://www.decanter.com)

HOTELS reviews hotels, focusing on those with more than 50 rooms. It also features articles on hotel management companies and major hotel chains. (http://www.hotelsmag.com)

National Hotel Executive is an online magazine targeting hotel owners, senior executives, and investors. Its features include hotel real estate listings, newswire, and industry events. (http://www.hotelexecutive.com)

Wine Spectator is dedicated to covering all aspects of wine, including its harvesting, producing, and branding. The magazine also covers stories about the hurdles involved in winemaking, including those caused by climate and other environmental factors as well as ineffective techniques. (http://winespectator.com)

Web Sites

Concierge.com offers online travel information. Concierge publishes original travel guides and recommends top hotels, restaurants, attractions, shopping, and nightlife for visitors. The interest and ideas section contains vacation ideas for every type of traveler. Budget, luxury, and adventure vacations are featured on the Web site. Concierge.com also offers travel tools such as map finders, destination finders, currency converters, and weather maps to help guests. Finally, Conde Nast magazine articles are also available. (http://concierge.com)

Foodservice.com is an interactive community for people in the food service industry. It offers job ads, equipment and supply links, franchising information, forums for discussion, and e-articles. (http://www.foodservice.com)

The FoodServiceWarehouse was founded in June 2006. Its goal is to equip foodservice operators with the tools and knowledge necessary in making their own businesses more successful. Shopping for foodservice equipment and supplies is made easier via "guides" designed to take buyers step-by-step through the process. The staff at FoodServiceWarehouse are called "product experts." They are certified foodservice professionals, accredited by the North American Association of Foodservice Equipment Manufacturers. The three-month CFSP training program works towards raising professional standards and encouraging continuing educational development among foodservice professionals. The online education center guides food service equipment buyers in their purchases. Foodservicewarehouse.com essentially offers a wide range of articles and research materials that will help any foodservice operator make better purchasing decisions. (http://www.foodservicewarehouse.com)

On the Cutting Edge

The Rise of Digitized Magazines

As with most other industries, periodicals in the hospitality industry are less paper-driven now that, in the information age, the up-to-the-minute potential for updating Web sites has enabled them to usurp the importance of their printed counterparts.

Gecko Hospitality "is North America's premiere hospitality recruiter," according to its Web site. Look here for postings of jobs in all realms of the industry. (http://www.geckohospitality.com)

Hospitality eBusiness is a full-service Internet marketing and direct online channel strategy firm. Hospitality eBusiness helps hoteliers to increase their business profits from the direct online channel and transform their Web sites to better serve their main distribution channels. HeBS services include Web design creation, brand development, strategic planning, industry research, and online media planning and buying. HeBS has created best practices in the industry. It also publishes articles about the industry frequently, and serve as guest speakers at many of the industry's main events. (http://www.hospitalityebusiness.com)

Hospitality Upgrade covers industry trends in the hotel, travel, and food service industries. (http://www.hospitalityupgrade.com)

Hospitality Jobs Online is a top site for hospitality jobs in hotels, resorts, restaurants, and clubs nationwide. It also offers career toolkits for job seekers, as well as advice for employers. (http://www.hospitalityonline.com)

Hospitality Publishers is a specialty publisher serving the hospitality industry exclusively. As of 2007, U.S. Hospitality has more than 2,500 hospitality publishing clients and an annual clientele of over 15,000 advertisers. Their clients include some of the largest hotel chains in the world, small independently-owned restaurants, tony beach resorts, major suburban apartment complexes, independent hotels/motels, visitor bureaus, condo/rental properties, and a host of additional hospitality venues. This site helps clients put their best foot forward with their customers by producing informative, eye-catching publications that also attract business for local advertisers. Some of their custom publications include: hotel/resort guest directories, keycards, TV Channel stands, menus, event/wedding planner guides, visitor guides, apartment/condo guides, etc. U.S Hospitality offers online products as well. (http://www.ushospitality.com)

Hotelmarketing.com is the leading online magazine for hotel marketers, hoteliers, and online travel marketers. Over 550,000 people sign on to HotelMarketing.com for their industry news and information. Its daily email newsletter reaches approximately 35,000 subscribers. HotelMarketing.com is updated daily and covers breaking news and business information pertaining to online travel, Internet marketing, and the hospitality industry in general. It is also available as an online magazine, daily email newsletter, or RSS news feed. Best of all, its content is free of charge to interested subscribers. (http://www.hotelmarketing.com)

Hotel News Resource contains links to various hotel resources, suppliers, trends, industry news, and trade shows. (http://www.hotelnewsresource.com)

MeetingsNet is the meeting industry's go-to site for information and resources related to planning meetings and events. (http://meetingsnet.com)

On the Rail is a thriving community for professionals in all areas of the restaurant industry. It is a valuable online resource for anyone who wants to know more about the industry and for those seeking a place that speaks their language. (http://www.ontherail.com)

Probrewer.com is a resource site serving all trades of the specialty beer business. Probrewer provides numerous tools and materials to assist a brewer in his or her endeavors within the beer business. The site offers information on the technical side of brewing filtration, yeast, tank and refrigeration information, as well as sales and distribution. (http://www.probrewers.com)

Sally's Place is the place to be for useful information and insightful commentary on food, wine, and travel. Offering more than 2,400 pages of content, it has everything the working (or aspiring) cook needs, from recipes to menu planning. (http://www.sallybernstein.com)

StarChefs is a Web site for the foodservice industry as well as those who follow food trends. Since 1995, StarChefs.com has identified and featured the best chefs in the industry, believing its mission to be the raising of the bar of food industry standards. Its job finder is considered one of the best online employment resources for those interested in careers within the hospitality industry. Star Chefs also offers hospitality companies marketing opportunities, market research, campaign development, site advertising, product sampling, event sponsorship, lead generation, and sponsorship placements. (http://www.starchefs.com)

Webtender is an online cocktail recipe database, guide, and encyclopedia of everything the working bartender needs. (http://webtender.com)

WetFeet provides insightful profiles of companies, careers, and industries in order to guide job-seekers toward the right careers, the right industries, and the right companies. Through their Insider Guide series and two Web sites, they help more than one million job candidates every year to perfect their interview skills, avoid making ill-fated career decisions, and add thousands of dollars to their compensation packages. (http://www.wetfeet.com)

Index

peaks and valleys, 120
perceived value, 120
performance appraisals, 53
periodicals, 135
personal assistant, 15
Pink Flamingo Hotel, 20, 22
Pittsburgh rare, 120
Planters hotel, 17
plating, 120
plats du jour, 71
point of distinction, 120
point of purchase, 120
Polo, Marco, 1
POS system, 120
Powers, Tom, 133
pow wow, 120
prep cook, 68–69
presentation, of food, 36
press release, 120
press trips, 120
prime interest rate, 121
private dining manager, 15
problem-solving, 89
Probrewer.com, 137–138
productivity, 121
profit margins, 53
prohibition, 11–12, 21
promotions
    employees getting,
        103–104
    in hotels, 89
    in restaurants, 91
property, 121
proxinoi, 2
Pullman, George, 13, 21
Pullman sleeper car, 13, 21

pump it out, 121
push it, 121

Q
quick services restaurant (QSR),
    121

R
racinos, 39
rack rate, 121
Radisson Hotels, 29
railroads, 13
Rainbow Room, 22
Raleigh Tavern, 8
ratatouille, 121
reach, 121
reach-in, 121
receptive operator, 121
Red Lobster, 36
redneck, 121
refer, 121
Regent Hotels, 29
registration card (reg. card), 121
repeat business, 121
reprimand, 121
reservation systems (automation
    vendors), 122
resort hotels and spas, 122
restaurants
    brief history of, 13–17
    China, 20
    Darden, 36
    Delmonico's, 13, 21
    early twentieth century, 13–14

WITHDRAWAL